Public Library Internships

Advice from the Field

Edited by
Cindy Mediavilla

THE SCARECROW PRESS, INC.
Lanham, Maryland • Toronto • Oxford
2006

SCARECROW PRESS, INC.

Published in the United States of America
by Scarecrow Press, Inc.
A wholly owned subsidiary of
The Rowman & Littlefield Publishing Group, Inc.
4501 Forbes Boulevard, Suite 200, Lanham, Maryland 20706
www.scarecrowpress.com

PO Box 317
Oxford
OX2 9RU, UK

British Library Cataloguing in Publication Information Available

Library of Congress Cataloging-in-Publication Data

Public library internships : advice from the field / [edited by] Cindy Mediavilla.
    p. cm.
    Includes index.
    ISBN-13: 978-0-8108-5186-3 (pbk. : alk. paper)
    ISBN-10: 0-8108-5186-5 (pbk. : alk. paper)
    1. Interns (Library science)—United States 2. Public libraries—Employees—
Recruiting—United States. 3. Library education—United States. I. Mediavilla, Cindy,
1953–
Z682.4.I58P83 2006
020.71'55—dc22

                                                                2006005935

∞™ The paper used in this publication meets the minimum requirements of
American National Standard for Information Sciences—Permanence of Paper
for Printed Library Materials, ANSI/NISO Z39.48-1992.
Manufactured in the United States of America.

Contents

Acknowledgments

$\mathscr{I}$ have several people to thank for making this book a reality. The first is Sue Easun, who suggested that I pull together a book about public library internships, a topic that has received little attention until now. Next are all the people who generously agreed to contribute chapters to this book: longtime colleague Bonnie Biggs, coworker Keri Botello, Denise Britigan, Christine Dettlaff, Davi Evans, Nancy Howe, Elyse Levy Kennedy, Janet Larson, Lori Lindberg, Penny Markey, Linda Matchette, role model Elaine Meyers, Natalie Munn, Jerome Myers, Nancy O'Neill, Michelle Ornat, Christie Peterson, Miriam Pollack, Kathy Sheppard, Dale Silver, Jill Stockinger, Alicia Sugiyama, teen librarian extraordinaire Erica Tang, and Taylor Willingham. I would be remiss if I did not acknowledge the advisory board who provided thoughtful guidance while I worked as project coordinator of the "From Interns to Library Leaders" (FILL) program. In particular, I want to thank Vicki Jenkins, Linda Wilson, and my supervisor Barbara Custen. Two UCLA students were especially helpful in gathering the articles for the literature review in chapter one: Ran Gust and Inna Ilinskaya. I also want to thank my editor, Martin Dillon, for his patient guidance through the production phase. And last, but never least, a big hug to my husband Tim Ahern for his unfailing support of my career and enduring appreciation of all librarians.

Introduction

$\mathcal{I}$n early 2001 I received a telephone call from Barbara Custen, then executive director of the Metropolitan Cooperative Library System (MCLS) in Los Angeles, asking if I would be interested in drafting a proposal for a Library Services and Technology Act grant. If awarded, the grant would allow MCLS, a consortium of public libraries in the Los Angeles area, to place library school students in paid internships in MCLS member libraries. Not only did I end up writing the grant proposal, but I was also hired to oversee the project during its first two years. Called "From Interns to Library Leaders" (FILL), the project proved to be highly effective at placing future public librarians in paid internships.

My attraction to the FILL project was natural. Although I am a library programs consultant for the California State Library as well as lecturer for the UCLA Department of Information Studies, my true passion lies in public libraries, where I worked for eighteen years before going elsewhere. I also believe strongly in the importance of internships as both a learning method and a recruitment tool. In fact, my first professional library job came directly as a result of working as a student intern at the Glendale Public Library in 1977. In those days, I thought I liked books a lot more than I liked people, but I soon saw the error of my ways when I was assigned cataloging duties as part of my internship. While the organized logic of the Dewey Decimal System did, admittedly, provoke a certain amount of fascination, I didn't really blossom as a nascent librarian until I started working at the reference desk. There I discovered the joys of information seeking and public service—a talent that my internship supervisor was (thankfully!) quick to note. As soon as I graduated from UCLA's library school, I was hired as a full-time entry-level librarian in charge of Glendale's service to homebound patrons. To this day, I remain grateful that my internship supervisor helped me realize my true calling as a public services librarian.

The goal of the FILL program was (and is) to place library school students in public libraries so that they, too, might realize their true calling as public librarians. So far, the project has been very successful at achieving this goal, with many FILL interns going on to become permanent librarians at their internship sites or other public libraries. Students who were initially lured by the monetary incentive of the program often convert to public librarianship after working at a branch or helping conduct story times. Even those who don't become public librarians remember their FILL experience fondly and vow to become public library advocates.

DEFINING INTERNSHIPS

So what exactly *is* an internship? At UCLA, an internship is defined as a "directed individual study related to work experience at the professional level" (*Student Handbook* 2004, 21). Students are placed in libraries or other types of information environments where they work with and observe practitioners. The internship—also called a "practicum" or "directed fieldwork" in some schools—is a structured experience, supervised by a degreed professional and monitored by a faculty member and/or program coordinator. Usually the student works for a requisite number of hours and may or may not receive course credit for the experience. Payment is not a requirement. Since the general purpose of an internship is to integrate theory with hands-on experience, most programs require that the student complete the school's "core" courses before registering for any type of fieldwork.

Although internships demand a lot of effort on the part of the student, the school, and the worksite, the benefits of such programs are overwhelmingly positive. Not only does the practicum allow the student an opportunity to put into practice new skills and knowledge learned in the classroom, but this experience may actually lead to one's very first professional job. In addition, the internship site gains an enthusiastic, if temporary, employee who often brings a fresh perspective to the workplace. Mentor relationships may also develop as new professional networks are formed. As the literature review (chapter 1) and individual narratives in this book reveal, a good internship can truly make a life-altering impact on one's early career.

ABOUT THIS BOOK

Sue Easun, then–acquisitions editor of Scarecrow Press, approached me about editing a book on public library internships after reading an article I wrote on the FILL project for *American Libraries* (June/July 2003). I agreed and, inspired by the first-person narratives included in Betty-Carol Sellen's excellent *What Else You Can Do with a Library Degree* (Neal-Schuman Publishers, 1997), decided to compile a book of firsthand "advice from the field" provided by former public library interns and internship site supervisors. Hoping for a diverse group of voices and representative experiences from around the country, I posted a notice on several electronic discussion lists, soliciting contributors who had either worked as or supervised a student intern in one of the many fields of public librarianship (e.g., public services, children's, technical services, branches). I also contacted people who I knew had expertise in specific internship areas—for example, Keri Botello, internship coordinator for the UCLA Department of Information Studies—and read what little literature on the topic was available.

As a result, I was able to collect eighteen chapters written by practitioners and library school faculty, who generously share what it's like to participate in a public library internship. I have also contributed two chapters myself: 1) a short literature review of real-life internship case studies, and 2) an assessment of the first two years of the FILL program. I was unable to recruit authors to address internships in technical services, nor did I find anyone to write about the legal aspects of student internships, although I do touch on this topic very briefly in my literature review.

The chapters described hereafter represent a broad spectrum of internship experiences—everything from handling typical reference questions in a traditional library setting to reaping the unexpected rewards of working on an American Indian reservation or in a prison library. Although some of the authors tell of instances that were more challenging than others, they all share an enthusiasm for experiential learning and providing the best public service possible. As is reinforced in the library literature, everyone involved in an internship ends up benefiting from the experience—whether it be a student who suddenly decides to become a children's librarian or a library director who appreciates the enthusiasm the intern brings to the worksite or the library school professor who is reminded of what is accomplished every day in the public sector. An internship is where classroom learning becomes reality.

The chapters have been arranged into four sections: part 1, "Developing Effective Public Library Internship Programs," where the nuts and bolts of five successful programs are revealed; part 2, "Traditional Public Library Internship Settings," where librarians and former interns discuss their experiences in reference, children's, young adult, and branch library internships; part 3, "Nontraditional Public Library Internship Settings," where surprising opportunities are found in literacy programs, archives, and public libraries on American Indian reservations; and part 4, "Using Internships as a Recruitment Tool," which recreates effective programs in Illinois, Los Angeles, and Miami–Dade, Florida. Each section is more fully described below.

PART 1: DEVELOPING EFFECTIVE PUBLIC
LIBRARY INTERNSHIP PROGRAMS

Following a brief literature review (chapter 1), representatives from the UCLA Department of Information Studies (chapter 2) and the University of Illinois Graduate School of Library and Information Science (chapter 3) describe what makes their internship programs so effective. According to Keri Botello, UCLA's internship program insists on cultivating the legacy of professionalism that was instituted in the library school more than thirty years ago. Today, the department prides itself on offering its students a diverse range of internship opportunities that are promoted at an annual open house event. Dale Silver, on the other hand, details the benefits of the University of Illinois's practicum program and the role each participant—student, site supervisor, faculty advisor, and practicum coordinator—plays in the process.

In chapter 4, Nancy Howe and Davi Evans enthusiastically share the elements of Santa Clara (California) County Library's highly successful graduate intern program, which incorporates a thorough training regimen. A more administrative view is presented in chapter 5 by Kathy Sheppard, who describes the rationale behind the development of Glendale (California) Public Library's internship policy.

As soon as Jerome Myers decided to go to library school, he then applied for a job with the Brooklyn Public Library, thus making him eligible for their internship trainee program. But as Myers quickly discovered, the library's trainee program had little to do with his school studies. He therefore approached library administration about creating a more fully integrated internship program. That program, known as PULSE (Public Urban Library Service Education), is described in chapter 6.

PART 2: TRADITIONAL PUBLIC
LIBRARY INTERNSHIP SETTINGS

Nancy O'Neill, of the Santa Monica (California) Public Library, provides a thorough list of things to consider when developing an internship program for future reference librarians. Her chapter is followed by Denise Britigan's description of the yearlong children's services internship she completed at the

Iowa City Public Library (chapter 8). In addition to helping with traditional children's programming, collection development, and other projects, Britigan worked on a statewide literacy program called Stories 2000.

Former UCLA student Erica Tang (chapter 9) shares how she boldly initiated a once-in-a-lifetime opportunity to intern at New York Public Library's recently renovated Teen Central. While there, she gained the confidence needed to become a young adult services librarian by helping develop the library's historical young adult collection and by interacting positively with teenagers.

The next two chapters are set in branch libraries, where the interns were treated to an array of professional experiences. In chapter 10, distance education student Michelle Ornat tells how a research trip to her local library ended up in her being offered an internship. She and her site supervisor, Linda Matchette, recall the experience. Christine Dettlaff's chapter, subtitled "How to Learn Thirty Jobs in as Many Days," tells of her whirlwind internship at the Pioneer Library System in Norman, Oklahoma. Not only did she gain a network of professional colleagues, but the experience led directly to her first professional library job.

The last chapter in this section is set in northern California, where the Sacramento City College places library information technology students in public library internships. Challenges faced by the students are related by the program coordinator Janet Larson and a librarian, Jill Stockinger, who hosts interns at the Sacramento Public Library.

PART 3: NONTRADITIONAL PUBLIC LIBRARY INTERNSHIP SETTINGS

Chapter 13 captures the complexities of interning in public libraries on two different American Indian reservations in San Diego County. As challenging as these experiences can be, Bonnie Biggs posits that the rewards of learning from a non-majority community are certainly worth the effort. Likewise, Taylor Willingham exposes the difficulties involved in providing literacy services and how such opportunities can help library students grow professionally. Examples of projects described in chapter 14 include the creation of a prison literacy center, coordination of an author/learner luncheon, and work on San Diego County's READ program.

The two remaining chapters in this section deal with archival internships. In the first, Lori A. Lindberg and Natalie Munn make an excellent case for placing interns in public library archives and local history collections. The benefits of such opportunities often include monetary compensation and the creation of strong mentor relationships. Phoenix Public Library's Center for Children's Literature is the focus of chapter 16, as told by youth services manager Elaine Meyers and former interns Christie Peterson and Alicia Sugiyama. During their internships, Peterson physically organized the library's collection of historically significant children's literature, while Sugiyama coordinated family literacy programs using the Center's rich assortment of materials.

PART 4: USING INTERNSHIPS AS A RECRUITMENT TOOL

Based on research showing that people usually enter librarianship because they have worked in a library or know someone who works in one, the North Suburban Library System in Illinois paired twenty undergraduate students with librarian mentors in 1991. Five of the students eventually went on to library school. Miriam Pollack, the author of chapter 17, coordinated the project.

A similar project was conducted in Los Angeles County, where federal monies were used to hire third-year college students to work in the library during the summer. As Penny Markey relates in chapter 18, these students were paired with children's librarian mentors in hopes that they, too, would want to become children's librarians.

A lack of strong public librarian candidates prompted the Metropolitan Cooperative Library System, in Los Angeles, to create "From Interns to Library Leaders" (FILL), a program to place library school students in paid public library internships. In chapter 19, I describe the elements that have made the program a continuing success.

Finally, Elyse Levy Kennedy concludes this section with an uplifting description of Miami-Dade Public Library System's intern/trainee program. The goals of the program are to create future library leaders as well as to provide staff paraprofessionals with an in-house career ladder. Success is measured by an increase of multicultural librarians who reflect the demographics of their communities.

I

DEVELOPING EFFECTIVE PUBLIC LIBRARY INTERNSHIP PROGRAMS

Library School Internships:
A Review of the Literature

Cindy Mediavilla

*W*hile there exists a relatively robust body of literature on academic post-graduate internships and "residencies," very little has been written about internships completed during library school. I have, therefore, attempted to collect here the handful of articles that capture the essence of effective student internship programs. Because so few articles focus specifically on public library internships, I have cast a net wide enough to include academic and special library programs as well. What they all have in common are the benefits gained by everyone involved in the internship experience. As Laura Claggett and her coauthors (2002) note, an internship "adds value, not only to the organization and the information center, but also to a student's success . . . everyone comes out a winner" (42).

INTEGRATING EXPERIENCE WITH THEORY

According to J. Gordon Coleman Jr. (1989), tension has always existed between library theory and practice. Originally taught by practitioners who doubled as teachers, course work took on a more theoretical flavor once library education migrated into academia. Although this move helped improve the quality of teaching, library training "now had to follow the academic model and, as such, became obligated to emphasize the theoretical and research aspects of the profession over its practical aspects" (Coleman 1989, 19). As a result, library school students began to complain about the lack of practical, experiential course work. To meet this demand, many library schools developed a fieldwork component as part of their curriculum.

Today, most library education programs offer their students the opportunity to experience hands-on fieldwork. This fieldwork, which tends to be closely monitored by a faculty member or staff coordinator, is usually called an internship or practicum. According to the most recent report of the Association for Library and Information Science Education, only three of the fifty-six programs currently accredited by the American Library Association do *not* offer fieldwork opportunities (ALISE 2003). However, as Norman Howden (1992) points out in his study of library school practica, little standardization exists among the programs that do offer fieldwork. In some institutions, like the University of Michigan School of Information, directed fieldwork is a required part of the curriculum (Holland 1998); in others, such fieldwork may only be taken as an elective. The amount of course credit a student receives for completing an internship or practicum varies by school, with some programs offering up to twelve units of credit while others apply no fieldwork credit whatsoever toward the master's degree (ALISE 2003). In addition, some library schools will not give credit for paid internships—a practice that might actually encourage libraries to violate the Fair Labor Standards Act (FLSA). As a recent article warns, any organization that benefits from the work of student interns should pay those interns at least a minimum wage. Schools and employers should clearly structure student internships as learning experiences that do not displace paid employees ("Are Your Interns Legal?" 2002).

Besides possible legal concerns, internships may also pose other problems, especially to the schools that must administer such initiatives. Faculty may be reluctant to add a practicum course to an already crowded curriculum or may wish to avoid the complications of overseeing such a time-consuming program. "Developing and maintaining a successful practicum program can be a considerable drain on an already tight library school budget, especially when site visits and faculty release time are considered," Coleman contends (1989, 20). Still, internships remain a popular part of many library school curricula and are filled with rewards for all participants.

BENEFITS TO INTERNS

For Christina Bennet (2004), undertaking an internship at the Indiana University–Purdue University Fort Wayne campus library was the highlight of library school. While there, she completed a series of projects, including working with the library's art history slide collection, compiling two collection assessment reports, presenting a workshop to library staff, and creating an online resource guide for patrons. As a result, she feels she gained an authentic yet broader view of academic librarianship.

Mary G. Wrighten (1994) also learned much about academic libraries during her internship at Bowling Green (Ohio) State University. Over the course of two years, she worked at the reference desk, gave library tours, cataloged and weeded the collection, taught bibliographic instruction classes, and served as cochair of the library's multicultural affairs committee. These various assignments "made the theory presented in library school come into much sharper focus" (62).

Describing her experience as a preservation intern at Saint Bonaventure University in Pennsylvania, Susan Mackey Frakes (1994) recalls that "it helped me to develop real understanding of at least some of the many issues [that] face librarians who are working to maintain their library collections" (8). In particular, she appreciated the opportunity to combine hands-on work with the critical examination of materials. "The internship taught me to challenge my own thinking," she relates. "I was encouraged to be creative and pragmatic, and yet, to recognize the limits of my own knowledge and skills" (9).

Claggett et al. contend that the "challenge to apply what [students] have learned, and then continue to learn by doing, can be very exhilarating." Calling such experiences "light-bulb moments," Maureen Malinowski remembers how theory became reality when she saw "the staff's commitment to meeting the customer's needs by providing information in the appropriate format and timeframe to bridge knowledge gaps and impact decision-making" (Claggett et al. 2002, 38). Likewise, Jennii L. Ramirez (1994), who interned as a roving reference librarian at the Diablo Valley (California) College Library, relates the thrill of overcoming "the anxiety present when first attempting to integrate classroom-acquired knowledge and library resources with a user's information need" (356).

The benefits of internships for library school students are many. As several articles point out, internships are especially helpful for career-changers and/or students who have never worked in a library before. In most cases, internships provide a nonthreatening environment where fledgling librarians can test their professional wings. Instead of proficiency, the expected norms are best effort and growth (Claggett et al. 2002; Quarton 2002; Roland 2000; Switzer and Gentz 2000). Wrighten (1994) mentions how grateful she was to do professional work as an intern without the added pressure of being vigorously evaluated as a librarian. Thanks to her internship, she was able to decide which area of library work best suited her skills and interests.

In my own article on the "From Interns to Library Leaders" (FILL) placement program in Los Angeles county, I describe the growth that occurs during public library internships. "I have been treated not merely as a student but as a colleague—a person who is trusted to carry a share of the load," Michael McGrorty explained during his stint at the South Pasadena Public Library. "This has been one of the most interesting and satisfying experiences of my life." For Natale Majkut, the experience was even more profound, drastically resulting in a career change from archives to public librarianship. Today Majkut works as a children's librarian at the Glendale Public Library, where she completed her FILL internship three years ago (Mediavilla 2003, 62).

Finally, the internship may provide students with their first chance to network with other professionals. Not only do interns build mentor relationships with site supervisors and coworkers, but some libraries encourage student participation on committees and in other professional development opportunities. Wrighten (1994), for instance, was named cochair of the library's multicultural affairs committee which, she feels, directly led to her being hired as the multicultural services reference librarian at her internship site. At Saint Bonaventure University, Frakes (1994) was invited to attend and make a presentation at the annual American Institute for Conservation conference. "[It] was an excellent opportunity to show other participants what I had been learning and doing at St. Bonaventure," she reports. "[And it] allowed [me] to see what other people in the field of preservation were doing" (9). Kristen Conahan Roland (2000) posits the advantages of introducing students to others who came before. According to Roland, "[A] network of former interns serves as an 'unofficial' professional association, automatically conferring the benefit of collegiality among peers that is often reserved for more structured organizations."

BENEFITS TO OTHERS

Of course, students aren't the only ones to benefit from the internship experience. As Claggett and her colleagues (2002) demonstrate, library schools gain much, too, by placing their students at various internship sites. Such programs force school administrators to form relationships with practicing librarians, often even leading to the hiring of practitioners as adjunct faculty. The school is viewed as progressive by the outside world and students benefit from an enriched curriculum. Internships enable faculty to mentor students into the profession and provide employers with prospective librarians who have the most up-to-date skills. Interns also enhance the learning experience of their fellow students by bringing practical knowledge back to the classroom. According to Diane Nahl et al. (1994), the "active learning environment" created by directed fieldwork enlivens the classroom experience and promotes greater student involvement.

The internship sites themselves also greatly benefit from the experience. Interns often bring "new ideas and insights that challenge conventional practice, which may lead to implementation of new and innovative processes, systems, and service" (Roland 2000). Quarton (2002) concurs, saying that "working with interns provides reference librarians the often enlightening opportunity to see their own jobs from a different perspective" (110). At the South Pasadena Public Library, reference librarian Michael Toman says that it is invigorating to re-experience the "exciting sense of librarianship" that originally attracted him to the profession. "It's been great having new library school students . . . coming in and bringing their fresh eyes and ideas," he admits enthusiastically (Mediavilla 2003, 62).

Libraries also appreciate having interns assume part of the staff workload, especially during bleak economic times. At the Manoa campus of the University of Hawaii, one hundred library school students provide some two thousand hours of public service a year at the library's information desk (Nahl et al. 1994). In North Carolina, the Environmental Protection Agency (EPA) library exists solely because of a long-standing partnership with the local library school. When the federal government cut the EPA's funding in the early 1970s, the dean of the library school at the University of North Carolina at Chapel Hill proposed that the library become a "working laboratory" for students interested in government and/or health sciences librarianship. Currently, the EPA library is staffed by three full-time librarians, one full-time library technical assistant, one part-time shelver, and a battery of interns. The interns are responsible for handling interlibrary loans, answering reference questions, cataloging materials, performing online searches, and managing the library's offsite branch. In addition to providing service to researchers, Roland (2000) feels the internship program increases the EPA's capital as a tax-supported organization by fostering the growth and development of future science and government librarians.

Indeed, one of the major benefits of internship programs is the growth of future professionals. In early 2001, Los Angeles area public libraries were suffering from what one newspaper called "a vexing shortage of librarians." The solution was to create a program, through the local public library consortium, to place library school students into paid public library internships. As a result, several graduates have been permanently hired by their internship sites (Mediavilla 2003).

This grow-your-own recruitment strategy has also been successful in Florida, where two public libraries currently groom staff to become librarians within their organizations. Since 1999, the Miami-Dade Public Library System has offered an intern/trainee career ladder to its paraprofessionals enrolled in master's-level library courses. Student interns work side-by-side with fully degreed librarians, learning the duties and responsibilities of a professional. Then, once they have completed half their course work, the interns are promoted to "librarian trainee" and begin to assume professional duties of their own. If the students choose to stay with the library, they are eventually hired at the librarian I level. To date, seven staff members have completed the program and are now librarians in the system (Kennedy 2004; Rogers 2003).

A similar project is flourishing in Broward County. Called the "Graduate Intern Program," the project allows staff paraprofessionals to receive on-the-job training in reference and children's and young adult services. Appointments are made with the understanding that the interns will enroll in a master's-level library program by the following semester and complete their degrees within five years. Over the past six years, fifty-one participants in the program have become librarians in the Broward County Library (McConnell 2004).

ELEMENTS OF EFFECTIVE INTERNSHIP PROGRAMS

So what makes an internship program effective? Switzer and Gentz (2000) admonish that interns must be treated as professionals as reflected in their salary, project assignments, and professional development opportunities. Moreover, Wrighten (1994) contends that internships should last long enough to allow students time to integrate theory with practice.

According to Kennedy (2004), the first consideration for most students is financial. In fact, internships that provide monetary compensation are preferred by students and employers alike. Paid internships tend to attract a higher caliber of candidates and students are able to devote more time and effort to the library. As Michael Toman explains about the FILL program, "since it's a paid internship, students who might not otherwise be able to do so can participate for the number of hours needed for a real sense of what it means to be a librarian" (Mediavilla 2003, 62).

Both the Miami-Dade and Broward county libraries provide multiple financial packages for their interns. Trainees and interns at the Miami-Dade Public Library System are paid salaries higher than those earned by their paraprofessional coworkers. In addition, employees are eligible for the county's tuition reimbursement program, which covers up to 50 percent of school costs. A scholarship is also available to pay for childcare, transportation, the purchase of a home computer, and other nontuition expenses (Kennedy 2004). In Broward County, tuition may be reimbursed up to $2,150 a year. The library's foundation also awards scholarships to cover nontuition expenses and has created an "accelerated" program that pays tuition above the amount reimbursed by the county. "If not for this scholarship, many students could not afford to move through their education program at a pace that matches their abilities," insists staff development officer Carole McConnell (2004, 35).

Along with a salary, interns should also be given professional-level assignments to complete. Switzer and Gentz (2000) warn against promoting a "student-worker" mentality and instead recommend that interns be given projects that contribute professionally to the organization. According to Bennet, assignments should result in tangible end products that can be added to the student's professional portfolio. "Be open with your supervisors from the start," she advises students. "Discuss your career goals, past projects, and areas of interest" (305). Wrighten (1994), Meiseles and Feller (1994), and Claggett et al. (2002) recommend putting internship goals and objectives in writing. "Each task, skill, or experience should have a purpose or goal," Wrighten explains. "The ultimate goal should be that the intern will leave with documented and demonstrated ability to perform agreed upon library skills" (65).

Most effective internship programs incorporate an extensive orientation that includes an introduction to the library as well as an overview of expectations. At the California State University San Bernardino campus library, interns undergo two weeks of orientation and observation before being allowed to work on the reference desk. This period includes four active learning modules: (1) an overview of the campus and its library; (2) an introduction to the reference desk; (3) becoming familiar with the library's catalog; and (4) using the most popular databases. Students are also given an orientation packet, including maps, campus information, and important telephone numbers, plus an intern handbook (Quarton 2002). At the Axinn Library of Hofstra University in New York, serials interns are eased into their jobs by sorting the mail first before learning how to check in periodicals. After they master these tasks, they then move on to tackling OCLC and the library's online access computer system (Meiseles and Feller 1994).

Wrighten (1994) began her internship at a branch of the main library—an experience that she says was ideal because it allowed her to enter library work at a "moderate pace." After her first semester, she was then transferred to the main library, where she was immersed in a series of assignments. Although many libraries rotate interns through various departments to provide maximum exposure to different job options, Switzer and Gentz (2000) caution against "schedule frenzy," where students are moved too quickly from site to site. In her experience as a roving reference librarian, Ramirez (1994) admits that helping patrons use the library's databases was a more comfortable way to start her internship because she had a much smaller "universe" to conquer than the entire reference collection. Similarly, Nahl et al. (1994) found that students who work at a library's information desk—as opposed to starting at the reference desk—feel "the satisfaction of immediate proficiency" by mastering a limited body of knowledge (294).

An important element in successful internships is reflection, where participants "articulate their actions and reflect upon them." If done correctly, this can lead "to an appreciation for the art, science, complexity and ambiguity of the profession" (Claggett et al. 2002, 41). In several of the case studies examined here, students were required to keep some sort of diary or written record of their experiences. Frakes (1994) kept a detailed notebook where she recorded questions, observations, processes, and techniques "in order to track my understanding . . . and to serve as a reference source later" (8). Likewise, Sue Feller was asked to keep a diary as part of her internship at the Axinn Library (Meiseles and Feller 1994). "Keep a notebook or journal handy," Claggett et al. recommend to interns. "Recap what you did and observed after every session, questions you have and ideas of what you would do differently in *your* library" (40).

Claggett and her coauthors (2002) also note that "an excellent mentor seizes the 'teachable moment' and recognizes occasions to share knowledge and to learn from each activity" (40). Not only do these more seasoned librarians share their extensive base of knowledge, but they should also help the student develop a support system of current and future colleagues (Switzer and Gentz 2000). As Wrighten (1994) recommends, each intern should have a mentor who will act as an advocate for him or her.

Mentor relationships are best nurtured when the intern experience lasts longer than a semester or school quarter. Wrighten (1994) worked as an intern for two years before being hired as a professional librarian. Feller interned at the Axinn Library for two semesters (Meiseles and Feller 1994), while Frakes (1994) worked as a preservation intern for Saint Bonaventure University for a year. Internships at the EPA library also take a year to complete (Roland 2000). Although public library internships typically conclude after one school term, the intern programs at the Miami-Dade and Broward County libraries each last up to five years. The longer the students are in the program, the more sophisticated their duties become until eventually they are hired as professional librarians (Kennedy 2004; McConnell 2003).

REFERENCES

ALISE Library and Information Science Education Statistical Report 2003. http://ils.unc.edu/ALISE (accessed January 5, 2005).

"Are Your Interns Legal?" 2002. *Library Personnel News* 15, no. 1/2 (Winter/Spring): 14.

Bennet, Christina. 2004. "Enhancing Your Internship: Add Value to Your Work in the Field." *College & Research Libraries News* 65, no. 6 (June): 304–5.

Claggett, Laura, et al. 2002. "Library Practicum 101." *Information Outlook* 6, no. 9 (September): 36–42.

Coleman, J. Gordon, Jr. 1989. "The Role of the Practicum in Library Schools." *Journal of Education for Library and Information Science* 30 (Summer): 19–27.

Frakes, Susan Mackey. 1994. "Preservation Internship at Saint Bonaventure University." *Conservation Administration News* no. 56 (January): 8–9.

Holland, Maurita Peterson. 1998. "Practical Engagement Programs: The 'PEP' at Michigan's School of Information." *Library Hi Tech* 16, no. 2: 49–54, 89.

Howden, Norman. 1992. "Practicums and Field Experiences." *Journal of Library Administration* 16, no. 2: 123–40.

Kennedy, Elyse Levy. 2004. "Miami-Dade Public Library System's Intern/Trainee Program." *Library Worklife: HR E-News for Today's Leaders* 1, no. 9.

McConnell, Carole. 2004. "Grow Your Own." *American Libraries* 35, no. 9 (October): 34–36.

Mediavilla, Cindy. 2003. "FILLing in the Public-Librarian Ranks." *American Libraries* 34, no. 6 (June/July): 61–62.

Meiseles, Linda, with Sue Feller. 1994. "Training Serials Specialists: Internships as an Option." *Library Administration & Management* 8, no. 2 (Spring): 83–86.

Nahl, Diane, et al. 1994. "Effectiveness of Fieldwork at an Information Desk: A Prototype for Academic Library–Library School Collaboration." *Journal of Academic Librarianship* 20, no. 5/6 (November): 291–94.

Quarton, Barbara. 2002. "Five Steps to an Effective Internship Program." *College & Research Libraries News* 63, no. 2 (February): 109–11.

Ramirez, Jennii L. 1994. "Reference Rover: The Hesitant Patron's Best Friend." *College & Research Libraries News* no. 6 (June): 354–47.

Rogers, Michael. 2003. "Tackling Recruitment." *Library Journal* 128, no. 2 (February 1): 40–43.

Roland, Kristen Conahan. 2000. "Training Future Science Librarians: A Successful Partnership Between Academia and the United States Environmental Protection Agency." *Issues in Science and Technology Librarianship* (Spring). www.library.ucsb.edu/istl/00-spring/article3.html (accessed December 15, 2004).

Switzer, Teri, and William Gentz. 2000. "Increasing Diversity: Programs and Internships in ARL Libraries." *Advances in Librarianship* 23:169–88.

Wrighten, Mary G. 1994. "The Significance of a Minority Reference Internship Program." *Reference Librarian,* no. 45/46: 57–66.

• 2 •

Library School Internship Programs: How UCLA Does It

Keri S. Botello

The internship program at the University of California, Los Angeles (UCLA), Department of Information Studies began under the watchful eye of dean Andrew H. Horn over thirty years ago, shortly after the school began offering a two-year master's degree. The program was designed to offer supervised professional-level experience to students in their second year of study. Dean Horn's careful planning and efforts to establish relationships with suitable sites, coupled with his close supervision of the program in its infancy, are some of the reasons for its continued success.

Today the internship program is an established and important part of the department's curriculum. Although not a requirement, approximately 70 percent to 80 percent of the students complete an internship before graduation. Currently, there are more than 250 individual internship sites available to UCLA students. In geographic terms, students may intern in sites as far north as Santa Barbara, as far south as San Diego, and from Santa Monica eastward to San Bernardino. The range of experiences offered is startling. Students may select from academic libraries, medical or law libraries, archives of all different descriptions—presidential, corporate, film, university, governmental, or private—or public libraries, school libraries, and news libraries, to list a few. They may also choose different media with which to work: film, manuscripts, books, slides, digital records, photographs, artifacts, ephemera, or sound recordings. The level and types of technology utilized by internship sites vary—interns have the opportunity to master new technologies or participate in a "low-tech" experience, if desired.

13

THE BASICS

Students enroll in the internship class, which has two parts: (1) fieldwork, where students work at the internship site for a set number of hours during the academic term; and (2) a classroom component, consisting of class meetings, written assignments, and an in-person conference with the internship program coordinator. Grading is based on completion of the required fieldwork hours as well as satisfying the classroom component.

A fundamental requirement of the internship is that students must be supervised by an individual with an appropriate professional degree. In most cases, this means a master's degree in library and information science (MLIS), but in some settings, such as an archive or museum, another degree or certification may be more appropriate. Because the site supervisor functions as the "instructor" for the educational/practical fieldwork, a common theoretical foundation is critical to the success of the experience. An effective site supervisor is one who blends practice with theory.

Students must also be assigned professional-level work, typical of a fledgling information professional, involving more intellectual activity and challenge than clerical tasks. In reality, however, "information" work often involves a mixture of both professional and clerical skills. This combination of intellectual exercise and detail-oriented "mind-the-store" tasks provides a dry run for starting a new career. What is described in the classroom, after all, does not always coincide with what really happens on the job. As frequently occurs, the meaning of the term "local practices" becomes clearer to many students by the end of the internship.

Mentoring is another major component of the practical experience and often offers the intern a glimpse at the larger professional world by sharing the thoughts, expertise, and wisdom of a seasoned information professional. An effective mentor not only provides an orientation to a specific information environment, but also presents an introduction to the larger information profession. In some cases, the mentoring relationship continues well beyond the conclusion of the internship.

Before enrolling in the internship, students must have completed the first year of the MLIS program, including relevant "core," or required, courses and several electives. In this way, the student acquires the theoretical and intellectual framework necessary to begin the internship. Site supervisors can be confident that the students have been exposed to fundamental information concepts and principles that should now be part of their mode of thinking and problem solving. Likewise, students expect that their intellectual preparation will be tapped, reinforced, and deepened through the activities, tasks, and projects completed during the internship.

THE REWARDS

The students are the primary beneficiaries of the internship program. The hours worked per week provide situational tests of the principles and theory previously covered in class or in required course readings. In some cases, the theory is reinforced or validated; in others, classroom learning proves inappropriate or not pertinent for the particular situation at hand. Equally important is the opportunity for the interns to begin developing their own philosophy or personal style as an information professional—this is only possible through "doing." There is no better time to test theory or pick and choose successful techniques or strategies gleaned from working with experienced professionals than during an internship. Fieldwork provides a protected, supportive environment where new things can be tried. Sites consider interns as professionals and expect the students to take responsibility for projects or programs. Interns are also asked, for the first time, to offer opinions, reasoning, and justification in the same way as colleagues.

Internships also offer the chance for students to explore one or more information settings, if desired, and/or provide interns with a longer, more intensive preparation for their chosen specialty. Not all "information-professionals-to-be" are sure they know in which niche they belong. The freedom to explore several options in order to discover a true calling, or gain more varied experience, is invaluable. Time spent following up on a newly sparked interest in archives or cataloging may uncover self-awareness that working at a public service desk is where one's heart truly lies—or may indeed confirm one's passion for archives or cataloging. Likewise, a yearlong internship at a busy academic reference desk may provide the confidence necessary for a "reference junkie" to succeed. A short eye-opening experience before graduation may prevent a serious career misstep later on.

Evaluation of the student's progress is part of the internship. At the end of the academic term, sites are asked to submit to the program coordinator a form assessing the student's learning and performance. The protocol for completing the evaluation and the degree of the intern's involvement in the process vary with the site. Some site supervisors confer with and counsel the intern before completing the form. Other sites ask the intern to provide feedback before submitting the form, and still others consider it a confidential matter to be handled exclusively by the internship coordinator. The evaluation is an opportunity for interns to receive more formalized feedback on their progress as measured against professional criteria. The process also demonstrates the variation in practice across institutions and exposes the intern to professional review procedures. When combined with the course grade, this feedback gives students a more complete indication of their promise in the professional arena.

An internship may lead directly to a first professional job after graduation, or sometimes even before graduation. More often, however, the experience offers a stress-free networking opportunity where dialogue between a novice and more experienced professionals can begin. Information professionals are a tight-knit but communicative group that likes to share information with colleagues of all levels. Friendships, possible project collaborations, or even a coauthored journal article may result from relationships begun during internships. At the very least, site supervisors may act as references during one's search for that first professional position.

The internship sites also reap rewards. By hosting an intern, the site remains in touch with what is going on or being taught in library school. Interns are eager to share what they are learning and to compare it to what is being practiced outside of the classroom. Experienced professionals often look to interns for advice on the latest technologies and sometimes even rely on them to train librarians and staff on newer applications or devices. In addition, there is great reward in contributing to the education of the next generation of information specialists or, as the case may be, future coworkers.

Host sites also benefit by having interns help during busy periods. Students often accomplish important tasks or projects that no one else has time to do. Asking an intern to complete a long overdue project that involves unwanted or uncomfortable change helps to shift the approach to the project, with the result that positive change can be made. Interns remind the rest of us why we became information professionals. Their energy and fresh outlook often inspire and energize others. Their curiosity motivates us to rethink or reconsider what prompted their questions.

HOW INTERNS FIND INTERNSHIP SITES

Making a "cold call" may be difficult for some people. It is even more difficult for an individual looking for work. One way the Department of Information Studies makes it easier for students to find an internship is by holding an annual "open house," bringing together host site representatives and potential interns in a less formal atmosphere. The open house is a "meet and greet" affair, including food and a high level of noise from all the folks talking to one another. Over a hundred people typically attend. Interns come armed with résumés and are advised to prepare a thirty-second speech summing up their skills and experience. They are also encouraged to wear comfortable shoes. Site representatives arrive with handouts and business cards, prepared to lure talented students away from competing internships. The event makes for a high-energy afternoon, filled with networking and conversation. Shortly afterward, follow-up calls are made and interviews scheduled.

All internship programs need to grow and change to stay in touch with the profession and remain a relevant part of the curriculum. UCLA students are encouraged to suggest new, possible internship sites. In some cases, interns seek an experience located closer to home, or one that fits a new interest initiated by a guest speaker or course readings. Keeping up with potential work sites is daunting. The students have been instrumental in the growth of our program. Their suggestions, along with faculty referrals and calls or e-mails from institutions requesting to become a site, all increase the opportunities available to our students. A directory of potential internship sites is available for students to use. In addition, the program coordinator is always happy to provide guidance and advice.

WHY IS THE UCLA INTERNSHIP PROGRAM SUCCESSFUL?

There are several reasons for the success of UCLA's internship program. First, it started with the careful planning and development of the program by Dean Horn so many years ago. He and others in the school scrupulously communicated the professional standards required of internship sites, and they upheld the requirement that students engage in professional-level work that complemented and more fully developed the theories presented in class. That standard is still in effect today. The internship program is an integral part of the education of information professionals at UCLA and is one of the reasons we continue to maintain a two-year curriculum.

The program is also successful thanks to the long-term commitment of the individual internship sites. Many sites have hosted interns since the program's inception. They all share the vision of Dean Horn, as well as that of the department, and continue the mission of our program: to provide a professionally supervised, challenging internship that is, first and foremost, an educationally based experience. The diversity of opportunities offered in terms of type of institution, range of geographic locations, and type of material with which to work all contribute to the success of the program.

The students, too, are another important reason for the program's success. Individually, each shapes the internship experience to prepare a career path and/or to learn more about a particular type of information setting. The students are assertive in crafting a practical experience that benefits them while serving the institution. They appreciate, most of all, the value of having a theoretical grounding seasoned with some hands-on experience before embarking on a professional career. Internships are proof positive of the value of information professionals to society. No matter the environment—the public library, an archive, an academic library—the intern learns about the individual community and witnesses firsthand how access to information improves people's lives.

• 3 •

The LIS Practicum:
An Internship with Academic Credit

Isabel Dale Silver

*F*ield experience is considered integral to the master's of science degree program of the University of Illinois Graduate School of Library and Information Science (GSLIS), which provides various enrollment options to students, including on-campus, online, and commuting. The LIS-591 practicum course provides students with the opportunity of supervised fieldwork, performing professional-level duties in an approved library or information center. The practicum—basically a short internship for academic credit— potentially benefits not only the student but all of the other major participants, including the site supervisor, the practicum faculty advisor, and the graduate school.

GSLIS has successfully integrated service-learning into its academic program, and the practicum course is one of several that provide experiential learning. Service-learning is based on the philosophy that to learn, students need to be engaged intellectually and experientially in real-world problems and situations. Service-learning is also based on an understanding that reflection is integral to the learning process and should have many avenues for expression in speaking, listening, and writing individually and in groups.

The practicum course aims to provide a bridge between classroom learning and real-world engagement, thereby making LIS education more relevant to students. While some of the other performance-oriented GSLIS courses emphasize community service and social responsibility in accordance with underlying service-learning tenets, the practicum course fosters—in addition to academic education and personal growth—a slightly different emphasis on professional development, participation, and conduct.

INTRODUCTION TO THE LIS-591 PRACTICUM

The practicum provides students with several opportunities to:

> gain new professional work experience, along with LIS training, knowledge, and skills in a wide variety of LIS settings;
> work with at least one or more experienced professionals;
> explore career options within the profession; and
> learn more about their own interests and abilities.

Although they are undertaken typically by regular on-campus students, many of whom lack prior LIS experience, practica are becoming increasingly popular with online and commuting students as well. While the online and commuting students tend to be employed full-time, often in library work, the practicum is increasingly seen by all students as an excellent chance to try out a different type of library or professional LIS work. This opportunity is also made available to the post–master's degree students in our certificate of advanced study program, although few of these students—who are, for the most part, working professionals—take advantage of this offer.

Through participation in the practicum course, the site supervisor and host organization gain additional staff, new ideas, enthusiasm, supervisory experience, and satisfaction with the experience of mentoring a new professional into the LIS profession. The practicum faculty are kept in touch with the myriad activities and challenges in the real world of library and information services, as they help students to plan and design a practicum experience. GSLIS also gains cross-fertilization with the real world of libraries and information, linking classroom theory and concepts with students' practical experiences and applications and site supervisor needs, enhancing the learning environment in the academic graduate program and the classroom.

One thing that the practicum is not is busywork. Students are not permitted to perform routine or repetitive work for the bulk of the practicum. If a practicum becomes routine after a time, students are encouraged to request greater responsibility or a wider range of duties at the site. Students are expected to acquire new experience and learning and for this reason may not perform a practicum in their current or previous place of employment. The following examples of practica descriptions, drawn from a recent semester, demonstrate a wide range of professional experiences:

> adult services in a public library, including reference services, collection development, and special programming;
> youth services in a university laboratory high school library;

developing special collections in academic and public libraries;

serials cataloging in an academic library;

website design and development;

reference and instruction services in a private medical library;

indexing in a special corporate library;

cataloging and processing special manuscript collections;

fostering literacy among special education pupils in an underprivileged
   public high school;

reference services in undergraduate and community college libraries;

reference services in special academic libraries, including law, medicine,
   social sciences, business, and others;

developing a research guide for a special library;

metadata creation for a digital library collection;

commercial database searching for private clients of a for-profit research
   center; and

acquisitions services in a large research library.

The goals of the practicum at GSLIS are to provide an opportunity for students to work in a professional environment under the supervision of an experienced librarian or information specialist and to provide students with an opportunity to integrate the theory and knowledge of course content with the application of principles and practices in a work environment. Students gain practical experience based on their understanding and application of theoretical knowledge by observing the analysis of and solutions to problems arising in professional work settings while interacting with colleagues in a professional work environment, participating in a representative range of professional activities in the work setting, and developing professional self-awareness.

THE PRACTICUM PARAMETERS AND REQUIREMENTS

The practicum course is available to all students who have completed at least fourteen hours of academic credit (equivalent to three and a half full-credit courses) in the forty-hour GSLIS program. While some students want to take a practicum relatively early in their academic program, the course prerequisite is essential. Students who already possess some basic LIS course credits are more attractive to site supervisors, who want their temporary helpers to be able to function at a professional level during their brief visit with the organization. Also, the course prerequisite enables students to draw on their relevant course work (e.g., reference, cataloging, information storage and retrieval, preservation, storytelling) and put it to work in actual on-the-job service, programming, and problem-solving situations.

The students must choose a practicum site that offers a new experience for them. In other words, they may not do a practicum in their place of employment (past or present) nor may they perform professional work with which they are already familiar. The aim is for students to gain new experience, working with professionals who are new to them, in a new setting to achieve optimum experiential learning. Another crucial factor of site selection is that the student work with an experienced professional, who therefore must have an advanced degree in library and information science or in a closely related field.

Scheduling the practicum contact hours is negotiated by the site supervisor and practicum student. Students must complete the course within the semester in which they are enrolled. They may begin the practicum earlier, however, with practicum approval from their faculty advisor and the practicum coordinator.

The practicum course requires students to spend one hundred hours at the work site. Although the practicum work site is usually a library, students are increasingly branching out to nontraditional sites, including online, private, or nonprofit information providers. Up to but not exceeding 25 percent of the on-site time must be spent working on a special project, which is related to, but different from, the ongoing work of the practicum. The special project is identified as finite in scope, and quite possibly results in a product or deliverable upon completion. Some examples of special projects recently undertaken by GSLIS students include:

> creating user guides to various collections, such as:
>> an instruction guide to a medical hospital library's electronic resources,
>> a guide to a human relations area file in a large research library,
>> a guide to resources and instruction for literacy development in a public library,
>> electronic annotated bibliographies of special collections, including children's books, electronic books, and Chinese language films, and
>> a pathfinder of marketing information for a customer;
> assessing the effectiveness of, and user satisfaction with, a commercial electronic search engine to assist in management software decision-making and allocation of resources in a special corporate library;
> updating, expanding, and enhancing a special library's electronic database;
> developing special collections, including evaluation and weeding in public, academic, community college, and special libraries;
> cataloging special collections, including digital collections;
> designing and creating websites;

evaluating, developing, and improving user interfaces to digital collections;

encapsulating fragile items in a rare special collection;

planning and implementing special youth programs, such as:

an anime (i.e., Japanese animated films) movie night,

a sixth-grade reading group for active readers, and

a book club for reluctant high school readers;

assessing use of e-mail reference service in a college library;

documenting librarian cataloging activities associated with a high-density storage facility of a large research library; and

assessing and evaluating the results of various Google search strategies (i.e., full-text, first-paragraph, and keyword-only) on a collection of Illinois state documents.

Increasingly with nontraditional or technical practica, the work itself is a "special project." In these cases, students are advised to develop another, smaller but related special project to meet the requirements of the course. They are especially cautioned to make sure the practicum work will not exceed one hundred hours or, if that is likely, to be sure that the site supervisor is aware that the practicum course is satisfied with one hundred student contact hours.

At the end of the semester, there is a required practicum focus group meeting, which provides students with the opportunity to reflect on their fieldwork experience and share these diverse LIS experiences with each other. Before commencing, a rule of confidentiality is invoked to cover all comments made within the discussion. This affords students the safety to speak openly and freely on what they discovered about a particular type of LIS organization, site supervisor challenges and problem-solving techniques in the day-to-day operations, strengths and weakness of the organization and its services, interesting aspects about the patrons, and most importantly what they discovered about their own likes and dislikes and capabilities.

Also, this closed session provides invaluable feedback to the practicum coordinator on course requirements and what advice to pass on to future practicum students. Overwhelmingly, the most frequent and repeated response from students is that "all students should do a practicum!" On the basis of their experience, it should be a required course. Feedback also includes suggestions on ways to improve the practicum process. It can also reveal a problem at a site, involving either the nature of the practicum work or the conduct of a site supervisor. Given our advance work to prepare site supervisors for their responsibilities, complaints from students are rare.

To complete the practicum course, the student must turn in any required papers, reports, or daily logs to the practicum faculty advisor, as well as any deliverables expected by the site supervisor. Requests from practicum faculty advisors to their advisees may vary, but the practicum coordinator advises all students to keep a daily log. The daily log is not an itemization of activities performed but rather a reflection on the personal and professional lessons of the day:

> What did I learn today?
> What "best practices" did I observe?
> What professional problem-solving did I observe?
> What did I learn not to do?
> What did I learn about myself: my strengths, my weaknesses, my likes, my dislikes, learning gaps? new courses? more experience needed?

Preparation of the daily log gives the student something concrete to take away from the practicum course—reflections of their first (or new) professional experiences, reactions, and challenges. These logs are also a help to the practicum coordinator, providing insights to help with advising and counseling future students. For example, they are a reminder that students tend to be initially nervous, intimidated, or even frightened about the site or about beginning the practicum. The logs also demonstrate the growth of the student from the start to the finish of the course.

Finally, the site supervisor prepares a written evaluation of the student to submit to the practicum faculty advisor, who then communicates with the site supervisor about the student's performance. Owing to site supervisors' requests, a standard evaluation form will be provided. After consultation with the site supervisor, the faculty member submits a grade of either "satisfactory" or "unsatisfactory" to the student.

ADDITIONAL COURSE FEATURES

There are some additional but optional features of the practicum course. The practicum coordinator also holds an initial class meeting (both on-campus and online) for new practicum students. If they haven't done so already, this provides a chance for all students to meet the practicum coordinator, who is their resource throughout the semester of the course. This meeting also enables students to meet each other and to hear about the various fieldwork experiences sought by other students, to talk together about goals and expectations, and to ask questions.

Another feature is a relatively new electronic classroom that includes the class roster, contact information, and bulletin boards. Originally created for ad-

ministrative purposes, this feature now provides practicum students with a uni-
fying classroom experience. The practicum coordinator uses this infrastructure
to send out notices regarding the course (e.g., deadlines and meeting dates) and
also posts questions for student response. The goal is to increase students' reflection about the field experience and prompt a deeper interaction with their
site supervisors. While the practicum is essentially the lone student "out in the
field," the electronic communication infrastructure enables students to read
about the experiences of others and to communicate with each other. Some
examples of bulletin board questions include:

> What are the personal goals and expectations for your practicum?
> What were some of your very first impressions about your work site (e.g.,
> about the library, the site supervisor, the ways of operating, the pa-
> trons)?
> What is your sense of the "cycle" or "cycles" of work in your organization—
> the ebb and flow of work in general and certain special tasks in partic-
> ular?
> What can you learn about the budget of your organization?
> What is the budget process?
> Who compiles it? Who approves it?
> What is the source(s) of funding?
> To what categories are the funds distributed? [Students are instructed
> not to reveal actual numbers and details, but rather to present sum-
> mary findings.]
> Are there any surprises here?
> Does the budget truly reflect your organization's mission?

While the budget question is very difficult, it potentially provides rich information about the organization, the support of its mission, the availability and
openness of information, the familiarity of the site supervisor with the budget
process, the sources of funding, and its allocation to various functions.

ROLES AND RESPONSIBILITIES

The practicum involves four participants, each with specific roles and responsibilities. These are:

> the student, who conducts the fieldwork and is responsible for setting it up;
> the site supervisor, who agrees to train, supervise, and mentor the practicum
> student;

the practicum faculty advisor, who counsels the student to ensure that the academic interests, professional needs, and career goals of the student are addressed in the field experience and who, in consultation with the site supervisor, submits the practicum grade; and

the practicum coordinator, who works with students and site supervisors to instruct on practicum rudiments and to facilitate a positive experience for all.

More specifically, the student is ultimately responsible for creating the practicum by:

identifying potential practicum experiences related to personal career goals and interests (often, this is the most challenging step for students);

exploring specific potential practicum sites and identifying site supervisors;

introducing the practicum to the potential site supervisor;

negotiating the parameters of the practicum with the site supervisor and the practicum faculty advisor (i.e., objectives of the practicum, type of work to be completed, work schedule, special projects); and

completing and submitting the required paperwork, most notably the practicum contract, to the practicum coordinator.

The site supervisor is responsible for contributing to the professional development of the student and, therefore, plays a key role in the practicum experience. Specific activities include:

negotiating the practicum contract with the student, including the provision of a realistic statement of expectations, an interest in the student's educational and professional needs, and basic information and procedures for starting work at the site;

scheduling the student's time and arranging for necessary work space, supplies, and equipment;

providing an orientation to the site and ongoing training, supervision, and development, which might include discussing cogent issues and challenges facing the organization;

working with the student to design a special project of value to both of them;

meeting with the student to discuss the practicum experience and progress at the site; and

preparing an evaluation of the student's performance for the practicum faculty advisor.

The practicum faculty advisor is ultimately responsible for ensuring that the student has created a carefully planned and meaningful professional experience that reflects both academic and professional integrity. The advisor does this by discussing the practicum with the student, assisting as needed, and approving the practicum. Specifically, the faculty advisor:

assists with and approves the initial practicum description;

assigns as necessary any supplemental readings or projects to enhance the field experience;

coordinates the evaluation with the site supervisor; and

assigns the final grade.

The practicum coordinator plays a significant role in advising and assisting both students and site supervisors. For students, the coordinator:

conveys the purposes, objectives, requirements, and procedures of the practicum course through individual advising and informational meetings for groups of students;

posts new and available practicum sites on a special, in-house electronic bulletin board;

advises students on creating a practicum, including consideration of their career goals, suggestions for sites, recommending practicum faculty advisors based on the LIS area of the practicum, and clarifying the administrative process of necessary paperwork;

establishes an electronic classroom with bulletin boards for announcements and reminders, and posts questions for student reflection and discussion;

schedules and presents an end-of-semester focus discussion group meeting, one on-campus and one online, for students to reflect upon and share their experiences; and

intervenes if a difficulty or misunderstanding arises between the major parties of the practicum.

Intervention is rarely needed. Student issues typically have included a preference for more or less structure, or a desire for more training and mentoring. These situations provide excellent opportunities for the students to manage and negotiate on their own. As a student once responded, with the tacit agreement of others, "I love that there was the assumption that we were 'out in the field' on our own, and that the practicum coordinator was fairly hands-off, though I knew I could contact her at any time if my placement was a disaster." Similarly, site supervisors might encounter the same kinds of problematic behavior they sometimes experience from regular staff, including tardiness, absence, and inappropriate dress. Likewise, this is best handled within the field site.

Problems or misunderstandings are rare because the practicum coordinator prepares both students and site supervisors for the expectations of each to the other. In addition, site supervisors are thoroughly informed about the purpose and objectives of the practicum, as well as the significant responsibility to mentor the student. In great part, the role of site supervisor is only undertaken by those willing to invest the additional time and energy to mentor a practicum student. The practicum coordinator:

>   contacts LIS professionals to recruit new site supervisors;
>   provides site supervisors with information about the practicum philosophy and goals;
>   invites all site supervisors—some experienced and some new—to a meeting (on-campus or via teleconference) at the beginning of the semester to discuss preparation for practicum students, training, and strategies for success;
>   thanks site supervisors in writing at the end of the semester for their contribution to GSLIS's academic program; and
>   administers the University of Illinois full tuition and fee waiver (TFW) granted to site supervisors as a gratuity for their service.

The TFW may be used for a term at any of the three University of Illinois campuses. Recently, GSLIS instituted an organizational TFW to those few external organizations that consistently supervise students. This enables the organization to bestow a TFW upon an eligible staff member or to create and supplement a graduate assistantship or internship.

THE PRACTICUM PROCESS

Although flexible, the practicum process should ideally be undertaken sequentially, one step at a time. Several resources are available to assist the student in this process, including the electronic practicum guide (available at http://www.lis.uiuc.edu/gslis/degrees/courses/practicum.html), which presents a description of the practicum course along with the student's responsibilities. Also included here are frequently asked questions, required forms, a comprehensive list of practicum sites that have hosted GSLIS students, and a list of practicum faculty advisors and their area of expertise. The practicum coordinator holds introductory meetings and meets with students on both an appointment and drop-in basis. Students also have an academic faculty advisor to consult.

The first step, which is frequently the most difficult, is for the student to decide on the type of experience most desired and, from there, identify the appropriate organization and site supervisor. Then it is up to the student to make contact with the potential site supervisor. The student may refer the professional to the electronic practicum guide, which has information intended specifically for site supervisors (http://www.lis.uiuc.edu/gslis/degrees/courses/supervisor_info.html). The practicum coordinator is also available for more information and advice. However, students typically are quite successful in this step, easily securing a site supervisor without much intervention by the practicum coordinator.

The student next secures a practicum faculty advisor who has a specific interest in the practicum field and can provide consultation on creating the fieldwork experience, thus ensuring academic approval for it as a course. The student then reconnects with the site supervisor to discuss more specifically the practicum activities and to complete the practicum contract (available at www.lis.uiuc.edu/gslis/degrees/courses/guide_form_2.pdf). This form, which is central to the process, articulates the student's objectives and rationale for doing the practicum. The form also requires a description of the practicum duties and activities, the schedule of work hours at the site, and a preliminary proposal for the special project. Once the contract is signed by the student, the site supervisor, and the practicum faculty advisor, it is then submitted to the practicum coordinator for final approval and permission to register for the course. Other required forms include a template for students to construct a résumé for potential site supervisors and a form to connect site supervisors with the tuition and fee waiver gratuity. The student also completes a special project abstract, which does not have to be turned in until almost midway into the semester.

Students frequently have questions about how to complete the practicum. To assist students, the practicum coordinator maintains contact with all practicum students by way of the class bulletin board and e-mail. Specifically, the coordinator:

> reminds students that the practicum must be completed by the end of the current semester;
>
> suggests ways for students to notify both their site supervisor and practicum faculty advisor to let them know that the practicum is nearing completion to facilitate the assignment of a grade;
>
> schedules a focus discussion meeting for students to attend either on-campus or online; and

reminds students to submit any reports or projects created within the practicum or required by the site supervisor and/or practicum faculty advisor.

ADVICE FROM PRACTICUM STUDENTS

As a result of the focus discussion meetings, valuable advice from students has been collected to pass on to future practicum students. Overwhelmingly, students declare, "DO A PRACTICUM, especially if you have never worked in a library. Experience counts." Additional advice includes the following:

"Choose your site supervisor carefully." (This is a testament to how much students recognize and appreciate the contributions of their site supervisors.)

"Pick something challenging. It may sound scary at first, but it will stretch you. Step outside of your comfort zone."

"Do something different." For example, "If you are interested in school libraries, consider a practicum in children's services in public libraries. You may discover that you are interested in both." (This advice applies to types of service as well, such as trying cataloging even if the goal is to become a reference librarian.)

"One hundred hours at a site is not enough." Therefore, "Know what you want to do and use your time carefully."

"Do a variety of different tasks."

"Choose a special project YOU are really interested in, especially one that you don't explore in depth in the classroom but want to understand before entering the 'real' world of work."

"Take advantage of the opportunities to observe and participate in other areas of the library (ask about working in a different department or doing outreach)."

"Be willing to request a practicum at sites that you don't think will be a possibility. You might be pleasantly surprised!"

"If you are feeling overwhelmed at first, let your site supervisor know." (While the first few days may seem daunting, students do quickly adapt and catch on. To feel pressure initially is a very common occurrence. Students soon discover that it quickly dissipates).

The scheduling of the practicum course and specific hours at the work site generate much student advice as well, such as:

"Do one at the end of your program because your course work really contributes to the practicum and your contribution to the site."

"Don't do one too late in the game because you might want to make academic program changes and take some other courses."

"Consider doing a practicum over the school break because the intense experience allows for rapid learning and growth." (It should be noted that faculty tend to advise students to stretch out a practicum over the course of the longer fall or spring semesters to enable maximum learning and to enhance interaction between field and course).

"Try to vary your work shifts. Work a morning, afternoon and evening shift, and spread them over the week." (This enables the practicum student to work with a greater variety of clientele, especially in public libraries where the volume of business and type of patrons vary greatly depending on the day of the week and time of day. It also enables practicum students to meet, work with, and observe a greater variety of professionals and staff.)

"For children's public librarianship, do the practicum during the summer term to experience the intense activity and readers' advisory challenges of the summer reading club."

Experienced students definitely urge other students to be pro-active in their practicum:

"Speak up at the work site to get the experience you need and want."

"Pump the librarian and other staff for tricks of the trade, learn about their individual philosophies, listen to their anecdotes."

"Ask questions!"

While students are working hard to be new professionals, they should also be encouraged to remain students, observing and studying how others conduct themselves, interact with patrons, and problem-solve.

BENEFITS TO ALL PARTICIPANTS

Given the additional responsibilities required of students, site supervisors, and faculty, is the practicum worthwhile? After all, students must take the initiative to create a practicum experience. Once there, they must invest effort and energy in dealing with new challenges and programs as well as nurturing relationships with their site supervisor and others. Plus, they must now balance time at work, home, and school. Others, too, are impacted by the practicum. Site supervisors are responsible for mentoring entrants into the profession, and faculty advise students over and beyond their regular teaching loads. The benefits, however, far outweigh the costs.

Although students are usually motivated to learn about a particular type of library while acquiring new skills, they may broaden their goals to use the practicum to:

> compare it with another type of information center with which they are familiar;
>
> learn more about their own strengths and weaknesses, and likes and dislikes;
>
> gain supplemental work experience to enhance their résumé and job search; and
>
> gain confidence in utilizing their LIS education.

Students tend to see the benefits of the practicum as far greater than their investment. The practicum coordinator rarely needs to "sell" the course; instead, practicum students tell others why they think it should be a mandatory course. Typical student feedback includes:

> "The practicum was an incredible experience—one of the most significant in my entire master's program."
>
> "I'd like to do one every semester, although this wouldn't be very realistic!"
>
> "It makes your course work come alive, especially if you haven't worked in libraries."
>
> "It's an opportunity to try out an area of LIS you haven't previously considered."
>
> "The practicum experience confirmed my career goal."
>
> "The practicum experience has given me the opportunity to revise my career plan."
>
> "Although I was really nervous at first, the practicum helped me to relax about making a major career change."
>
> "The practicum has given me so much confidence!"

Furthermore, listing practicum work experience on one's résumé may help in the job market by providing an additional edge over the competition. The professional confidence one gains is also important and is bound to transfer over to the job interview as well as to the start of a new job. In fact, in many cases students have been offered permanent positions at their practicum sites.

While the experience is never promoted as a direct route to employment, students are encouraged to complete the practicum with at least one or more glowing references. The site supervisor/student relationship may also provide a good model for establishing and working in mentor relationships.

Like the exhortations from students that everyone should do a practicum, experienced site supervisors also praise the experience. Many of them see mentoring a new colleague into the profession as an opportunity to: pass on hard-earned experience that is frequently not conveyed in the classroom; provide a meaningful, valuable, and enjoyable experience for the student; shape and acculturate a new colleague; and, ultimately, contribute to the profession. At the same time, seasoned professionals may gain supervisory and management experience otherwise lacking in their jobs.

Site supervisors may use the practicum to justify a new position, try out a potential facet of a new position, or even recruit employees. Some practica do indeed lead to a paid internship or job offer, although students are not encouraged to expect a job offer. In these instances, site supervisors capitalize on their investment by extending the relationship with the student.

One of the most significant benefits occurs when site supervisors report that they have learned much from their students. Oftentimes, they receive new ideas and skills and a new way of looking at their organization. Typically, the practicum student comes to the site with enthusiasm, eagerness to learn, and a willingness to ask questions and make suggestions. In addition, practicum students may actually train the site supervisor in new technical skills, such as Web design and development. Students may also provide valuable feedback and insights about the work site, if the site supervisor creates a safe environment for this to take place. In short, reciprocal learning and mutual benefits frequently occur, prompting new site supervisors to say that they would welcome any future GSLIS practicum students.

While the practicum advising creates an additional workload, faculty too benefit from their participation in the course. For one thing, a practicum advisee brings the real world of library and information science to both the faculty member and the classroom. Increasingly, students are returning with experience from nontraditional and unique information sites, thereby broadening the world of knowledge. The practicum also provides faculty with an opportunity to better understand the students—their career goals and the professional jobs they are likely to pursue. Faculty also have the opportunity to make contact with the site supervisor, helping establish and maintain relationships with professionals in the field. Overall, the practicum course creates a bridge between the ivory tower and the workplace, enabling faculty to evaluate the effect of their teachings in the real world and allowing both realms to contribute to each other's programs, needs, and goals.

ISSUES FOR FURTHER CONSIDERATION

Several issues concerning the practicum course might be explored in greater depth. These include the elective nature of the course; the amount of academic credit granted; the requirement that the practicum must be in a field setting new to the student; and the requirement and nature of professional supervision.

Although the LIS-591 practicum is an elective, most students who take the course exclaim that it should be required of all. Certainly, the proponents of service-learning across disciplines are making a strong case for its educational value. If service-learning, or performance-oriented learning, is as efficacious as studies suggest, the elective nature of the course might be reconsidered.

The LIS practicum course specifically requires that students create a field experience in an entirely new setting. Given the elective nature of the course, this is both possible and acceptable. If the practicum becomes mandatory, however, greater flexibility might be requested by students. Also, the experience that students bring to the program might be considered eligible for credit.

Students occasionally voice the opinion that, comparatively, the LIS-591 practicum course is at least equivalent to a regular four-hour course. The university, however, has decreed that the practicum—because of its experiential nature—cannot be considered equivalent to a full-credit academic course. If experiential learning is as valuable as studies—and students—suggest, the amount of course credit might be a topic for reconsideration, especially in the professional disciplines.

As students increasingly work in nontraditional sites, the requirement of professional supervision becomes problematic. Some requested sites do not have on-site professional supervision, or the site supervisor is a professional in another field. If academic programs recognize the value of true experiential education, as different from on-the-job training, a broader definition of fieldwork might develop.

Finally, it should be noted that, while these issues do arise, the LIS practicum course as described is overwhelmingly considered a success in performance-oriented LIS education.

Santa Clara County Library's Graduate Library Intern Program

Nancy Howe and Davi Evans

The Santa Clara County (California) Library has operated a successful internship program for local students in the San Jose State University (SJSU) School of Library and Information Science since 2001. The goal of the Graduate Library Intern Program is to expose students to the field of public librarianship, as well as to the Santa Clara County Library. The program adds a practical perspective to the more theoretical learning provided by the university. The focus is on general reference, which includes adult, teen, and children's work. Students learn the foundational principles, policies, procedures, and organizational structure of the Santa Clara County Library. In addition, they learn how to conduct reference transactions, including reference interviews, search strategies, and readers' advisory techniques. Each internship consists of concentrated training at our administrative office for three days and shadowing at a community library, followed by four weeks of sheltered reference experience, and the option at the conclusion to become an hourly reference substitute at all of our community libraries.

THE PLANNING PHASE

Each library implementing a paid internship program faces unique planning and personnel issues. For Santa Clara County Library, the planning phase had two components: (1) the personnel logistics; and (2) securing organizational support for the program.

Civil service rules influenced the intern job descriptions, including minimum qualifications, classifications, and the salary range. In addition, we needed bargaining unit agreement on the broad issue of using interns within the workplace. Library administration designated one program manager to whom all interns would report and an initial budget for training the first group of interns. The budget was based on seventy-two training hours per intern. We also contacted the local library school, San Jose State University, to define how the paid internships would be different from the existing practicum program that also places students in libraries. While both programs provide practical on-the-job experience, the practicum is project-based and unpaid and the student receives course units for one semester. The library's internship, on the other hand, is a paid, ongoing employee relationship that focuses on reference training.

Most importantly, a successful internship program is totally dependent on internal organizational support. Securing the necessary level of support meant clearly communicating the goal of the program and unequivocal direction from our administration that all community libraries would participate. From the first day on the job, we wanted the interns to feel special and to be treated as professionals. They would be trained on professional-level responsibilities and would be mentored by our more experienced librarians. To help accomplish this, the program manager attended service group meetings of our managers and librarians to explain the program and get feedback. The county librarian welcomed the interns on their first day. After their initial training, we invited the interns and managers from the community library where they would be working to a reception where we all shared why we wanted to become public librarians. This set a collegial tone and launched the program on a very positive note. Ongoing communication and feedback from evaluations between on-site supervisors at the library and the program manager are essential.

RECRUITMENT AND SELECTION

To recruit students from the nearby SJSU School of Library and Information Science (SLIS), we post a job announcement on the county library's Web page and on SJSU SLIS's electronic discussion list. Pertinent information includes: program goal and description, salary, training description and schedule, qualifications, contact person, and date by which to respond. Our current employees attending library school are also encouraged to apply. Because of the reputation and success of our program, the interns themselves provide us with word-of-mouth exposure. The timing of the recruitment can be crucial. Too close to the start of the semester may cause confusion between the internship we offer and the program offered at SJSU; too close to the end of the semester, the students are busy with finals. The logistics of scheduling the staff and training facilities must also be considered.

Once a list of interested applicants is created, all candidates are contacted by telephone. The intern position is explained first, and then each student is asked about his or her expected graduation date. It is recommended, though not mandatory, that due to the length and structure of our internship, only those students who expect to graduate in a year or later apply. It *is* mandatory, however, that the candidates attend all training session dates and have a flexible enough schedule to be available to work on-call once the training is successfully completed. Candidates are asked to bring in a completed Santa Clara County employment application and a copy of their transcripts and grade point average. A date and time for the interview are then scheduled. Sample interview questions include:

> Please tell us about your educational and work experience.
> Why do you want to become a librarian?
> What are your career goals?
> Describe the most challenging class you have taken at library school.
> You are working on the reference desk with an experienced librarian and you hear her give incorrect information to a patron. What might you do?
> What makes a good reference librarian? Why do you feel you would be a good reference librarian?
> Tell us about a book that you have read for pleasure so that we will want to read it, too.
> You've suddenly been given a school assignment that is due in three days. You are scheduled to work at the library the next three days also. What would you do?
> What are your expectations for this position?
> Schedule issues: If hired, can you attend all of the training sessions? If you are hired and added to our extra-help roster, at what locations are you willing to work? Schedule conflicts?

What are we looking for in our intern candidates? Practically speaking, they must meet the employment needs of the library, be able to attend all training, and be flexible enough and available to work and still meet their school schedules. Most importantly, we are looking for demonstration of a strong customer service ethic: approachability and potential for excellence and leadership in the field. Once the interns are trained and on-call, they can expect to work in any of our ten locations—children's and adult reference desks—during peak times, in the larger or smaller community libraries. So they must be adaptable, with a desire to learn. And we look for any special skills the intern would bring to our organization (e.g., international language ability).

TRAINING

The seventy-two-hour intern training begins with a new employee orientation. Orientations are offered three to four times per year for all new library employees. We schedule the internship training to coincide with our next orientation. The goals of the four-hour orientation are to welcome new employees to the Santa Clara County (SCC) Library, confirm their decision to work for this organization, and present them with an overview of the values and structure of the county library before they begin working at an individual branch. A variety of guest speakers present information and the facilitators make sure all participants realize they are a valued part of the organization. Specific learning outcomes include:

being able to identify which libraries are part of the SCC system;
understanding the library's mission and values statements;
becoming familiar with the purpose and composition of the library's joint powers authority;
becoming familiar with the staff organization chart and how the employee's position fits in the organization;
understanding the different responsibilities of main staff classifications;
learning how the system is funded;
becoming familiar with how materials are received and processed;
becoming familiar with the library's bookmobile service; and
understanding the purpose of the literacy program.

After the new employee orientation, the specialized intern training begins. The training has two main parts: (1) centralized training; and (2) sheltered reference training at a community library. The centralized training is conducted over four days in a highly interactive format. We have two lead trainers who facilitate the entire session and a variety of specialized guest trainers who make presentations. The training room is located at our administrative headquarters and has white boards, movable tables and chairs, computers, an LCD projector, and a place for refreshments.

A cornerstone of the training is the binder we give each participant, "Starting Out: A Handbook for Librarians, Interns, and Library Assistants." It contains seven chapters, with well over a hundred pages of practical information. Not only is it used for the training, but it is also designed for the intern to use on our reference desks. The intern keeps the binder and personalizes it with notes. One small tip to trainers: Be sure the binder is paginated for quick reference during training and flag pages that need regular updating. Lead trainers have the same binder, with a copy of all handouts and exercises included, to simplify preparation on the day of training. The binder is organized as follows:

1. Introduction: Mission, values, history, organizational structure, finances, key facts, and descriptions of the community libraries.
2. Policies and procedures: Summaries and copies of key policies and procedures that apply to reference work.
3. Collections and services: Collection plan, description of special services such as the literacy program and bookmobile.
4. Reference and readers' advisory service: Policies, procedures, forms, and a list of reference books to know, developed by our librarians.
5. Catalog: Training materials for our online catalog.
6. Communication: Instructions for our telephone system and e-mail.
7. Community libraries: Maps, directions, floor plans, and a list of things to find out before working at the reference desk of a particular library (e.g., where is the pencil sharpener?)

We have found that it is important to start the centralized training with an icebreaker that goes beyond the library world. Usually participants and trainers introduce each other and include personal interests and hobbies. The group bonds quickly. Because the policies can be dry and involve a lot of lecturing, we cover them first. Hands-on exercises and small group discussions are interspersed throughout the training. Some of these include discussions around actual questions related to policies—for example, What would you say to a mother who asks if her child can get a library card without her permission? Others involve reference interview role-playing and readers' advisory questions that are answered from reference books located in the training room—for example, What can you suggest to a fourth-grader who is waiting for the next "Captain Underpants" book to come out? We also pose questions that can be answered by exploring the library's website—for example, When are children's story times?

After sixteen hours of training, the students are sent out to "shadow" at a community library. The intern contacts the supervisor to schedule a mutually agreeable four-hour shift to be completed prior to the last day of our centralized training. Usually this is within a one-week time frame. Each supervisor has been notified prior to the assignment and sent a copy of the shadow guidelines. The four-hour shift includes:

an orientation;
one hour on the adult reference desk observing an experienced librarian;
one hour on the children's reference desk observing an experienced librarian; and
completing a collection worksheet that requires the intern to locate items in the collection and answer related questions.

During the shadowing period, the intern, who wears an "In Training" button, observes only, rather than answering reference questions. Reference and readers' advisory interview techniques, search strategies, patron interaction, and customer service are all observed while the prior centralized training is reinforced.

This experience is then followed by another four hours of centralized training, giving the students a "safe" environment in which to comment on their observations. Intern comments have included:

"The librarian was able to search so fast on the computer."
"The library was so busy."
"The questions were difficult and there was such a wide variety."
"After being so sure I was interested in either academic or adult reference in a public library, I loved the children's room—it was so surprising to me!"
"The children's librarian knew every book in her collection, even when the child couldn't give her a title or an author and could only describe the book."

The interns also ask questions about what they have observed at the real-world public library reference desk. We have found that some interns have no work experience or course work related to public libraries, so we stress reference interviews, readers' advisory, and other practical aspects of the job. The learning outcomes for the centralized portion of the training include:

Understanding the main elements of and being able to apply the following policies to reference transactions:
privacy and confidentiality
Internet use
circulation

    community bulletin board
    community meeting rooms
    patron behavior standards
    chain of command
    staff and patron injuries in the library
    patron complaints
    county code of ethical conduct
Learning the following personnel policies and procedures:
    breaks and meals
    timesheets
    paycheck distribution
    computer access and passwords
    emergencies
Understanding and applying reference service policies
Knowing how to juggle multiple patrons
Conducting thorough reference interviews
Knowing several sources for readers' advisory services
Knowing when and how to complete a subject request
Introducing lists developed by the adult and children's reference staff
Becoming thoroughly familiar with the library's online catalog
Being able to instruct patrons on how to access the Web and Microsoft
    Office
Understanding and being able to explain the materials selection policy
Familiarity with the collection and the collection development plan
Knowing how to handle donations to the collection
Completing the interlibrary loan form correctly
Using the library's telephone system correctly
Knowing how to read and send e-mail
Competence in using the library's various databases and ability to instruct
    patrons on how to use them

"SHELTERED" REFERENCE TRAINING

At the conclusion of the centralized training, each intern is assigned to one of the community libraries for forty-eight hours of "sheltered" reference experience. During this time, the intern moves from just observing to actually handling the reference transaction independently, with a mentor librarian nearby. In addition to the hours on the reference desk, the intern has a meeting with the community library supervisor to discuss what it is like to manage a library and also observe a story time and other programming aspects of children's librarianship. (We have been pleasantly surprised at the number of students who convert to children's librarianship at this point in the program!)

A set of these guidelines is given to both the intern and the host supervisors. The supervisors are expected to complete the following checklist:

Orientation
- Using the "Things to Ask the First Time You Work at a Library" checklist, the adult and children's supervisors provide an orientation specific to their library and demonstrate the types of questions to ask in advance of working on a library reference desk in the SCC system.

Reference
- Intern is scheduled for at least twenty hours on the children's reference desk and twenty hours on the adult reference desk, with an experienced librarian serving as coach.
- First two hours per desk are observation, with the intern asking questions of the librarian, followed by eighteen hours of handling reference transactions, with the adult and children's supervisors or experienced librarians observing and coaching on reference interviewing and search strategies.
- Intern examines and writes annotations for the titles on the list of "Most Used Reference (Juvenile and Adult) Books."
- Intern explores the reference sites on the library Web page.
- Intern tests at least five of the subscription databases.

Story Time
- Intern observes one story time.

Management
- Intern meets with the community library supervisor for an overview of library management.

Progress Reports
- Adult and children's supervisors at the library send weekly e-mail to the program manager regarding the intern's progress with specific comments on reference interviewing, search strategies, and knowledge of sources.
- At the completion of the third week or thirty-six hours, notify the program manager, who will schedule a meeting with the intern at this time.

At the conclusion of the sheltered reference segment, there is an assessment of whether the intern is ready to work as an "on-call" substitute for the Santa

Clara County Library. The job classification of "graduate library intern" continues until graduation and, for some students, this means they will have two years of relevant employment to add to their résumé.

EVALUATION

Evaluation occurs at three points in the program: (1) a written form after the new employee orientation; (2) a written form and learning objectives checklist at the conclusion of the centralized training; and (3) an individual interview when the intern has completed the sheltered reference training. The program has evolved based on the feedback we have received.

In a real sense, the intern program is "owned" by every participating student, past and present. Their ongoing suggestions have shaped the program and kept it true to its original goal of providing a realistic, relevant introduction to public librarianship. The training agenda has never been the same twice. Each time we tweak the format based on their comments. For example, we added to the shadowing experience a "scavenger hunt" where they searched for the answers to questions related to the types of collections in our libraries. The hands-on experience of trying to find an easy-reader book was more illuminating than any amount of lecturing. Another change occurred when a couple of interns voiced concern that they needed more time to practice using our computer catalog, so we rearranged our training schedule to provide more time for an additional practice exercise. An intern asked more questions about public library funding and governance at her evaluative interview after completing the sheltered reference. As a result, we now periodically invite the interns to attend a meeting of the joint powers authority, our governing board, followed by a discussion with the program manager and a community library supervisor.

To the extent possible, the program is tailored to the needs and interests of each intern. The program manager meets individually with all the interns to discuss their experience and future learning goals. We try to expose them to the full spectrum of public librarianship. Monthly meetings continue between the interns and the program manager until they graduate from library school.

BENEFITS

The benefits of the intern program are very difficult to quantify because they have been so plentiful and far-reaching. It is a proven recruitment tool: to date we have hired three interns as librarians. We have brought in diverse talents and skills that were lacking in our organization, from language abilities to subject and technical expertise. The intern program has raised the bar in our reference work, turning every librarian into a mentor and teacher of the profession. We have become more conscious of modeling excellent reference skills and articulating our values when an impressionable intern sits next to us. After training, the intern becomes a source of substitute staffing for our busy reference desks.

From the intern's perspective, actual, professional-level experience may be added to the intern's résumé. The interns are exposed to a variety of positions in the public library and gain a better idea of their own career goals. Our library becomes a fertile training ground when the intern needs a project or research for a library class on public relations or collection development, to name just two. As one intern commented, "This internship training is the best class I've had at library school." The intern program is mutually beneficial to the students and the Santa Clara County Library and ultimately to the profession itself.

• 5 •

Creating an Internship Policy for the Glendale Public Library

Kathryn Sheppard

$\mathcal{A}$ new librarian at the Glendale (California) Public Library, who had interned with us before accepting a full-time position, asked me recently why our library chose to sponsor two to four master's of library and information science (MLIS) interns a year. I thought about this and replied that we enjoy having new library professionals around to remind us of the reasons we (older staff) became interested in the profession. We *are* an aging staff, with retirement on the near horizon. Many of us have been in this business for twenty years or more. We have seen plenty of changes in our own workplace, tasks, and tools. We have prepared mission statements and participated in strategic planning, and we can articulate very well the importance of libraries to individual users and to our communities. But we don't often reflect on why we ourselves chose to become librarians. Interns remind us of this—in fact, they sometimes ask us point-blank why we like doing what we do! It prompts us to take a minute to recall, and feel good about, the career decision we made years ago.

Interns are good for us and for our library in other ways. Many are coming to librarianship as a second career, bringing fresh viewpoints from previous employment and contributing colorful and very often valuable insights to our work processes. Their skills may be fresher than our own in many areas, because they have been more recently learned. Having interns at our library gives us a sense of helping to build our profession, of molding new librarians into providers of excellent service. We also benefit from the traces of scholarship and leading-edge research that attend our interns, reminding us that good minds drive our profession to reinvent itself time and again. Professional reading sometimes waits unread in the inbox, but conversation with a new librarian or intern brings us news we may have missed from the academic world and assures us that thoughtful colleagues are working through the issues and creating, perhaps, new approaches to the services we provide.

A RENEWED INTEREST IN INTERNS

Interns in past years were referred to us by library school professors. Or, they took the initiative, walked in, and asked to perform their internships in our library. They were assigned to public reference desks, conducted story hours, weeded the collection, and developed bibliographies, or were placed in front of cataloging terminals (or typewriters, depending on the era). Interns attained the hands-on experience they needed and were generally well liked and recognized by library staff. These interns were not paid, but often they hung around beyond the internship and got hired. A short internal written procedure was issued to document the circumstances under which an intern could become paid staff. That brief statement was the totality, in print, about internships at our library for many years. The process of taking on an intern remained on the casual side, and individual managers supervised their interns in individually different ways. We made no statement of the benefits of internships to the library and to the public we serve. We lacked a policy to guide the conduct of the internship, to set goals or recommend activities, and to provide for any special focus for an intern's professional interests. In the 1990s, budgets began to shrink and we became overwhelmingly busy—too busy to feel good about taking time to schedule and supervise interns. Our interest in sponsoring internships languished for some years.

The FILL ("From Interns to Library Leaders") program for southern California libraries came along in 2001 and revived our interest in taking interns. A Library Services and Technology Act–funded project of our regional library consortium, the Metropolitan Cooperative Library System, FILL appeared just at, and in response to, a time when the ranks of librarians were beginning to thin. Job applicant pools were emptying and library school enrollment had become worryingly low. FILL revitalized our interest in internships by providing a structure: Interns were centrally recruited by means of website listings, assigned to libraries in a fair and organized way, and (appealingly) were paid by an external body. FILL was designed to motivate master's of library and information science (MLIS) candidates to seriously consider beginning their careers in public libraries.

Participating in FILL obliged us to take a hard look at internships offered by the Glendale library. Our recent interns have had higher expectations of this vital part of their educational process. Some are second-career professionals, many of them used to a highly charged and time-sensitive work environment. These interns are excited about their new chosen profession and eager to get started. They need and deserve a more informed and planned approach to their time spent with us.

Some of our managers wanted to know how to work with interns more effectively. They had questions about the experiences they should be offering their interns. What library staff meetings should interns attend? Do interns benefit from working shifts on the circulation desk? Can interns work directly with children and, if so, need they be fingerprinted and officially documented, in line with the city's procedures? Before we developed a library-wide administrative policy, answers to these and other questions tended to differ from manager to manager.

Our library director, responding to a request for an interview from one of our interns, began to think about how our library develops and conducts internship offerings. She asked a few questions, was not entirely satisfied with the responses she received, and determined that it was time to improve upon our relaxed approach. She directed staff to develop goals, activities, and a written policy to guide future internships at the Glendale Public Library.

DEVELOPING AN INTERNSHIP POLICY

A task force, as a subcommittee of our managers group, was formed to identify the issues and put together a draft policy. These managers either had worked with interns over the years or had a current intern project in mind. They had a stake in making internships work more effectively and a warm interest in improving the interns' experience with us.

What did the Glendale Public Library want to offer its interns? And what did we as a library need in return? We identified several issues:

> How should Glendale internships be structured so as to help interns make the decision to become public librarians?
> Is it important for all interns to gain hands-on work experience with the public?
> Should interns be expected to contribute real assistance to the unit to which they are assigned?
> What are the processes, including required city requirements, for accepting an intern?
> Having brought interns into our "family," we do generally like to hire them when possible. How is this accomplished?

Our written policy needed to answer these and other questions as well as identify legitimate and meaningful internship activities.

The task force was set to work, broadcasting first a request for feedback from library staff, managers, and current interns about internship experiences from all of these points of view. The few simple guidelines used in the past were brought out and reexamined. Our director's wishes were consulted. Most of the group's work was conducted through e-mail in the interest of saving time, which proved an easy way to propose and make changes as the document grew.

It is always a challenge to develop guidelines that both serve well as specific procedures and are general enough to cover many potential situations. Happily our task force found the language needed without much debate. Our work resulted in what we believe to be a reasonable statement of policy and an easily followed procedure, now included in the Glendale Library administrative policy manual.

Several statements defining internships and their origins open the policy, followed by five assertions about internships at the Glendale Public Library. These answer the general question of what internships are designed to accomplish for the library and for the intern.

A list of mandatory activities for all interns follows. These incorporate hands-on tasks, areas of training, and other activities serving as a checklist to assure that basic requirements are met. As career librarians ourselves, we found it quite easy to draw up a list of skill-building experiences we felt would be most useful over the long term for a public librarian.

The task force determined that all public library interns need to work directly with the public to some extent, even if the intern's eventual career is to be in a behind-the-scenes support activity, such as cataloging. It is critical that MLIS candidates considering public library employment gain an understanding of the needs and demands of the general public and the role of the library in meeting those needs. And, while it is assumed that principles of good customer service are an integral part of the message received in the library school classroom, these principles are worth repeating more than once.

A second set of optional activities allows a manager, in discussion with a potential intern, to choose work areas best suited to the intern's personal interests and employment goals. These "electives" may be in specialized units or facilities of the library, such as teen services, community relations, conducting Internet workshops for the public, or grant preparation. The intern gains real work experience and is better able to determine if this specialty is indeed the one he or she is best suited for in future employment. The profession overall benefits from members who have given sufficient and serious forethought to their own individual strengths, weaknesses, and long-term personal goals.

The task force spent some time discussing the fact that it is important for our own library to benefit from internships as well, while not becoming overburdened by them. Managers must not undertake to supervise an intern at very busy times, when their workload does not permit adequate attention to the intern's activities and performance. Also, since interns are often assigned to work closely with staff librarians, it is important to assess the impact of the intern's schedule on the entire work unit. These considerations were not ultimately written into the final policy but are in fact generally understood by our managers when they are deciding whether to sponsor an intern at any particular time.

The task force discussed the importance of an intern's general understanding of how the public library fits into the picture of public service in local government, in terms of funding streams and specific community roles of the library. Interns should have an opportunity to observe the decision-making process within the library as well. It is often useful for persons entering the profession from other fields to understand the typical public library organizational structure, often quite different from other corporate structures. The task force determined that interns may attend unit and departmental meetings as appropriate but that a hands-on introduction to the wider context of government was probably beyond the scope of a ten-week internship. Interns are, however, encouraged to discuss these relationships and structures with their managers and peers.

The final internship policy, included here on the following pages, is succinct and unambiguous, providing guidelines and specific procedures to help managers design and supervise internships in their units.

Glendale Library Internship Policy

Internships at the Glendale Public Library [GPL] fulfill a requirement of the master's degree program in library and information science at UCLA [University of California, Los Angeles] and at San Jose State University. Internships are generally conducted in the second year of a degree program. Library school students may request an internship at GPL through the California state library's FILL ("From Interns to Library Leaders") program, or independently. All internships are coordinated through the senior library supervisor at the central library.

Internships generally involve about one hundred hours of work time (approximately ten hours per week for ten weeks) at a library site. A site manager works with the intern to find a schedule that works well for the site and for the intern.

Interns hired through the FILL program are paid through that program. If the student comes to us independently, the internship is on a non-paid basis.

All interns are considered volunteers and must be registered as library volunteers.

Once the internship is complete, the intern may be paid as a student librarian if funds are available and there is a need for additional staff. Additionally, any individual in library school who has completed twenty-four units may be hired as an hourly librarian if he or she meets all other requirements and if the library has a need.

GPL offers MLIS students a well-rounded internship grounded in practical experience. GPL internships are designed to:

fulfill the intern's educational requirement;

enable the intern to observe and understand the workings of the public library environment;

give the intern hands-on experience with core public library services and operations;

provide meaningful focused activities in the intern's specific area of interest; and

provide the library with valuable assistance in conducting programs, implementing projects, and performing core services.

While participating in a defined set of activities based on the intern's interests, interns also have the opportunity to explore other areas of public librarianship. The intern works with his or her supervisor to arrange opportunities to meet with, observe, and work alongside professional and/or support staff in any area of the library. Mandatory intern activities:

Tour all Glendale Public Library sites.

Receive instruction in use of the OPAC [online public access catalog].

Work at least one shift on a central library reference desk (adult or children's) and at a branch library.

Have an opportunity to observe circulation operations. If the internship is primarily conducted at branch libraries, the intern may receive more instruction in and hands-on use of the automated circulation system.

Have an opportunity to observe the library's internal decision-making processes in order to gain an understanding of how each department of the library fits into overall library system operations. Interns accompany their supervisor to at least one staff meeting, which may include the circulation advisory team, reference advisory team, central library advisory team, branches or children's teams, etc., as appropriate to the goals of the internship.

Optional intern activities (as relevant to the goals of the internship):

May participate in the collection development process. Participation may include bibliographic searching in the OPAC or vendor database, collection building activities, weeding, preparing booklists, or other tasks.

May observe technical services functions and may have an opportunity to perform some technical services functions.

May participate in public program planning and implementation (story hours, public book group, or other).

May observe and participate in some aspect of community relations/library promotion operations.

May gain some experience with library webpage evaluation and/or creation.

May observe and/or participate in library literacy efforts.

May observe and/or participate in public computer and Internet training.

May participate in implementation of library grant-funded projects.

• 6 •

Insider Training

Jerome L. Myers

In library school, we are taught about reference services, archives and conservation, cataloging, readers' advisory, and other topics. These courses are intended to provide us with the opportunity to learn about the services and operations of a library and to fulfill the requirements for our educational degree. Many library and information science (LIS) schools offer a variety of electives, such as government documents, public libraries, online databases in the social sciences, and young adult services.

What library school does not necessarily prepare us for is how we can apply this newly acquired knowledge to real-life situations working in a library. Many students would benefit from taking this knowledge and putting it to practical use. Professional degree programs, such as the health sciences or business administration (MBA), have always offered areas of specialization that require hands-on experience. MBA programs, for instance, often require their students to participate in an internship at a major corporation. This is not necessarily the case in library schools.

BROOKLYN'S LIBRARIAN TRAINEE PROGRAM

I was fortunate enough to discover a librarian trainee program at Brooklyn Public Library (BPL) and so applied there at the same time I applied to library school. I was accepted to both programs and knew my career in librarianship was off to a good start.

My first day on the job, I was introduced to staff and the layout of the library—the book stacks and public access computers. The library, a recently renovated tri-level, was in a remote area of Brooklyn. The modern interior gave the impression that the city was making major changes to the old run-down, dimly lit facilities that many of us "new breed" of librarians remember so vividly from elementary school.

As a librarian trainee, I was given a list of duties expected of a library school student. This list included weeding and reading the shelves, processing periodicals, and a number of other tasks that were not familiar to me from my library school curriculum. When the librarian schedule was developed, I was assigned to the reference desk for the first of many one-and-a-half hour shifts. Since I was new and experiencing my first library job, a librarian at the branch spent a few days sitting beside me at the desk assisting and providing tips on how to handle reference questions. I tried to apply what I had learned in my reference services class to the real-life job but, at times, it was a frustrating experience.

I spent several weeks learning about the library's collection. Certain parts of the collection, such as the international language books, nonfiction, and videotapes, were especially emphasized. The first few weeks at the reference desk were difficult. I did not feel properly trained or adequate for this part of the job. Users would come to the library throughout the day and approach the information desk inquiring about a variety of topics. "Can you tell me the birthplace of Albert Einstein?" "What were the Seven Wonders of the Ancient World?" "Where can I get the environmental impact report on the new mall to be built on Jamaica Bay?" Library users also requested copies of magazines or newspapers that were held in reserve behind the information desk. It was difficult to research and provide answers to their questions. Where were the resources we had learned about in school? In addition, the library subscribed to a set of databases that we never reviewed in library school. I had hoped that the Brooklyn program would provide on-the-job training to teach me how to apply what I had learned in school. After all, I *was* a "librarian-in-training."

Several months passed and I advanced through my LIS education. It seemed that what I had learned in class provided me with little or no value on the job. Many of the library's procedures remained a mystery to me. Even though cataloging is required in most LIS programs, seldom are we responsible for cataloging a book, especially in a large urban public library. I began to wonder who did the cataloging and where it was done. Did the library have a telephone reference department and, if so, how are questions answered? How did books arrive in the library? How were the books processed after they arrived and who orders the books?

I could have easily asked the librarian for the answers to my questions, but instead I decided that I wanted to learn about the library from an inside perspective—to gain a sense of how a large urban public library system works and acquire practical experience in the services it provides to the community. I began to wonder if it was possible to experience different areas of the library. Could I spend some time in the cataloging department or in telephone reference as a librarian trainee? What better way to apply what I was learning in library school than actually having the same job experience at the library?

As I soon learned, however, such an opportunity did not exist at BPL. Librarian trainees were not allowed to "experience" the various library departments. I was disappointed and so started talking with my peers. At that point, there were over twenty-five librarian trainees at BPL from various library schools in the area. Many of them felt frustrated by not being able to get a true sense of what it was like to be a librarian. What was the value of being trainees if we couldn't apply the theories learned in school to a realistic experience? The librarian trainee program was not providing the skills and training necessary to perform or advance on the job. In many academic institutions, library internships provide practical experience in administrative and adult reference services, as well as in selected areas such as collection development, library instruction, and technical services; yet these were opportunities denied to us.

After meeting with the other students, I decided to approach the library's director of the Office of Neighborhood Services about our concerns. The idea was straightforward: A trainee should receive in-depth practical training similar to an apprenticeship, where one would learn all aspects of working for a large urban public library. This training would complement as well as supplement the education received in library school. As the trainees advanced through their studies, they would gain practical experience in corresponding library departments.

REVISING THE PROGRAM

As a result of our discussing these issues with library administration, it was decided to revise the trainee program. The library's human resources department was especially concerned about recruitment and retention issues. In a large urban library system like BPL, it is often difficult to attract new librarians to positions that require a lot of effort for little pay. The librarian trainee program was an alternative to hiring newly degreed librarians. Applicants had to be enrolled in a master's of library and information science program. After completing a specific number of academic credits, the trainee's pay would increase until eventually reaching the starting salary for a new librarian.

Developing a program that provides proper on-the-job training for library school students was imperative to retain and recruit librarian trainees. Without proper training outside of the classroom, new librarians are often not prepared to deal with real-life situations. Creating an on-the-job curriculum, in which the trainees would learn all aspects of library services in an urban public library, was crucial to preparing future leaders in the profession. In addition, this experience would provide a solid foundation for students to explore the various career opportunities in a public library.

Creating a new trainee program for the library was a challenge. Organizing librarian trainee focus groups was vital to the design of the program. It was apparent that the trainee experience lacked structure. The connection between the theory taught in class and the practical component typically encountered in the library was nonexistent. Learning about collection development in school and then having the opportunity to develop part of a collection was one area the revised program hoped to address. Other areas included library administration and children's work. Although library management was a required course, many trainees did not feel qualified to be in charge of a library. Likewise, many felt inadequate conducting youth programs when they had no proper training as children's librarians.

As soon became apparent, staffing lines would have to be revised if this new apprenticeship-type program was to work. Most of the trainees filled librarian positions and so could not be reclassified; therefore, designing and restructuring the existing program posed an organizational challenge. The employees union was concerned that library staff would have to be relocated in order for the program to work. According to the union contract, librarians cannot be involuntarily relocated from one work site to another. Since the program required students to rotate among locations, it became apparent that some librarians might have to move to make room for the trainees. Furthermore, the trainees, who also worked under the same contractual guidelines, had to be declared exempt from the "involuntary" transfer clause. After several meetings with the union, it was agreed that they would be permitted to transfer among locations. However, a librarian could not be involuntarily transferred as a result of trainee placement.

It is important that the trainees learn about and experience the entire library system from both the public and nonpublic perspectives. This includes conservation and preservation, marketing, fundraising, cataloging, and library administration. In the new program, librarian trainees work side-by-side with senior staff members. They also participate in job exchanges throughout key areas of the library, spending at least three months in one particular area in order to be properly trained in that specialty. Emphasis has shifted from *doing* the job to learning *how to do* the job. This is the foundation of the new trainee program.

A NEW PROGRAM EMERGES

The new three-year librarian trainee program offers graduate students in library and information science the opportunity to receive practical training in urban public librarianship. The program, which was created to prepare future library leaders, provides opportunities to:

gain exposure to and experience in many of the concepts, skills, and technologies that are shaping the future of the public library and information fields;

examine current issues and trends affecting the public library and information fields; and

prepare for future leadership roles in traditional and nontraditional settings in the fields of public librarianship and information science.

Enrollees move through the program in three distinct phases. Phase I (year one), the librarian trainees receive training in all components of library operations, which are divided into several different functional units. These units vary in length and topics and may include:

- management
- administration
- collection development and management
- organization of information (cataloging)
- BPL technology
- document delivery
- preservation and conservation
- customer service training
- services to special populations
- community outreach
- programming and planning for agency service
- communication and promotion
- school outreach
- project management, research, and evaluation.

Training is done through workshops, lectures, discussions, and selected hands-on experience. A weekly e-mail newsletter is sent to the trainees and is intended to provide tips and on-the-job resources. The e-newsletter, called "Tomorrow's Librarian—Desktop Librarian Trainee Development," has proven to be a great success.

The new program provides formal and structured job exchange opportunities that allow the trainee to work in a variety of public and nonpublic service departments on short- and long-term projects. During this phase, the librarian trainee gains experience in other community libraries within a cluster and works with the manager of library services in each age-level specialty.

The second year, phase II, focuses on library administration and management as well as the central, business, and reference libraries. During the first part of this phase, librarian trainees work in a branch cluster and focus on individualized projects related to community library programs and services. They then experience public and nonpublic service job-exchange opportunities at the central, business, and reference libraries. The purpose of phase II is to create a self-directed course of study and to meet the challenge of interpreting results for decision-making in a public library environment.

Phase III, the final year, provides an opportunity to develop skills and gain experience in working with librarians, administrators, and system developers to design and implement information services and programs that contribute directly to accomplishing the library's mission and vision. Upon completion of this phase and in conjunction with completing the master's degree in library and information science, the librarian trainee is placed as a librarian within the Brooklyn Public Library system.

SUCCESS THUS FAR

With the support of library administration, the librarian trainee program began in fall 2003. The success of the program has been documented by trainee evaluations received from each participant at the completion of the designated three-month job-exchange rotation. The program participants are also required to keep a portfolio of any program materials relevant to their individual job-exchange experience.

The trainees have stated that the program has been beneficial in providing them with new opportunities to expand on the material learned in library school. The side-by-side working relationship with senior librarian staff has provided a much-needed mentorship for the trainees. Furthermore, monthly seminars, called "Books, Bytes and Brunch," provide the trainees with additional learning opportunities on relevant topics, such as "Government Affairs in the Urban Public Library," "Growing Leadership in the Public Library," "Community Outreach," and "Conservation and Preservation."

GROWTH OF THE PROGRAM

In 2004, Brooklyn Public Library and the Pratt Institute School of Information and Library Science received a joint Institute of Museum and Library Services grant to expand on the librarian trainee program. Called PULSE (Public Urban Library Service Education), the program offers Pratt students the opportunity to undergo either a three-year work/training apprenticeship at BPL or a less intensive 150-hour practicum. As part of PULSE, the library also serves as a satellite campus, offering new courses and enhancement seminars taught by BPL and Pratt staff.

There are currently twenty-five students enrolled in the PULSE program. They benefit from a class cohort system, where they have a chance to interact on an intensive basis with peers experiencing similar training and using the same academic curriculum. The theories studied in the classroom (e.g., collections, managerial skills and working with various populations) are correlated with on-the-job experiences, connecting theory and practice.

II

TRADITIONAL PUBLIC LIBRARY
INTERNSHIP SETTINGS

· 7 ·

Internships in a Public Library Reference Department

Nancy O'Neill

$\mathcal{I}$t sounds easy, exciting, even flattering. The internship coordinator considers your department a good training ground for future reference librarians and the interns are anxious to work there. Internships may indeed be exciting and flattering, but they require commitment and hard work if you are to succeed in providing benefits for the department and the intern.

BENEFITS OF INTERNSHIP PROGRAMS

Internships present rewarding partnership opportunities for everyone involved; moreover, they inspire learning in the library as well as in the student. Reference librarians usually enjoy teaching and sharing their experience and ability. In fact, training interns often reminds us just how skillful we are. On the other hand, an intern's fresh view may stimulate constructive change. In addition, internships provide the library a chance to develop a close professional relationship with the local library school. Such relationships may encourage staff to pursue continuing education or provide assistance in employee recruitment.

For their part, the interns profit from the knowledge of experienced staff and from a look into the "real world" of reference work. Most of us know that it is one thing to read about the reference interview and quite another to actually interact with a client. There is no substitute for practical experience in every aspect of reference work. Interns see the best practices of a diverse staff and learn to meld the theoretical with the pragmatic. Moreover, they may develop professional relationships and discover mentors. Through the internship, library school students develop confidence in their ability to function as a member of a team and as a responsible colleague.

DESIGNING AN INTERNSHIP PROGRAM

Before establishing an internship, you should consider the reference department's situation—do the library and staff support the idea of an internship program? Is there a plan in place? Where does the department need and want interns? Are there tasks and services appropriate for an intern to handle? Busywork does not result in a satisfying learning experience, nor should the intern be treated simply as free labor.

Decide who will have overall responsibility for the internship program. Usually this task falls to the head of reference, but in very large departments there may be sufficient supervisory staff to assign the responsibility to another librarian. Although it is vital that one person oversee the internship program, rotating the responsibility provides an excellent training opportunity for supervisory staff. In smaller departments, a similar opportunity may be provided by assigning responsibility for day-to-day intern supervision to various staff members.

The coordinator of the internship is responsible for communicating with the student and the library school, as well as overseeing the intern's training, and evaluation. A team approach to training can be very successful, but there should always be one person responsible to see that the program is carried out and that the intern achieves the desired experience.

Creating a checklist and timeline for coordinator duties helps keep the program running smoothly and assures that all tasks will be completed. A coordinator's checklist may include:

> attending internship fairs and/or advertising the internship;
> designing the internship program and training materials;
> conducting an assessment interview to determine the intern's skills;
> ensuring that the intern receives orientation and training materials;
> creating a schedule that is compatible with departmental needs and the intern's availability;
> providing a desk or office space with equipment and supplies;
> discussing and coordinating with the intern a particular project or set of tasks that are to be accomplished during the internship;
> designating a specific librarian to serve as the day-to-day contact or as a mentor if the coordinator does not serve in this capacity;
> informing library staff about the internship and the intern's duties;
> seeing that the intern is introduced to staff throughout the library, including library administration;
> providing regularly scheduled feedback to track progress; and
> evaluating the intern and the internship.

The coordinator assigns staff who are able to commit themselves to working with an intern. Mentoring has advantages if the librarian has the time and ability to devote to the intern. In smaller departments, the coordinator and mentor may be the same person. In larger departments and/or where the mentor and coordinator are not the same person, the mentor should be cognizant of the coordinator's checklist and take the opportunity to informally discuss each point with the intern to verify that she or he understands and is comfortable with each step. Mentors may provide role modeling, coaching and guidance, feedback, friendship, and a sense of belonging to the department.

The team approach is also an effective training mechanism that, in addition to distributing the work evenly among staff, provides the opportunity for each reference librarian to interact with the intern. Advantages of the team approach include: varied role models, discouraging dependence on one person, creating a wider network for the intern, and distributing the responsibility and opportunity for skills enhancement among staff.

An intern job description should be developed. Because internships are educational, the job description should focus on what interns will do during their time in the reference department and on what they will learn. If the library has internships available in various departments, the job descriptions will help prospective interns choose the one that best suits their needs. Such job descriptions are also extremely useful when attending internship fairs sponsored by educational institutions and/or when advertising the opportunities offered by your library.

Always interview the prospective intern to assess that person's skills and interests. The process should be similar to interviewing a prospective reference librarian so that the department and the intern are certain their objectives are compatible. The interview also provides the intern with experience that will be useful in future job searches. Interview questions may cover:

    prior library or reference experience and/or experience working with the public;
    why the student is interested in this particular internship;
    the student's career objectives;
    special projects, classes, or experiences that are applicable to reference work;
    special abilities or skills, e.g., language fluency, computer skills;
    the student's philosophy of reference work;
    knowledge of reference interview techniques;
    possible internship projects of interest; and
    objectives for the reference department internship.

Be sure to assess the intern's skills before assigning a project or tasks. The reference desk assignment will probably be the most important part of the internship, but the student should not be treated as free desk help. If she or he has had no reference desk experience, the department may wish to concentrate on training and keep other projects to a minimum. On the other hand, if the intern has had some experience and/or is skilled in the use of reference resources, the department may wish to direct more time to a project.

If direct public service is the primary objective, then assign the intern to all reference stations, including telephone and virtual reference services, if at all possible. The intern's skills may not be adequate for telephone and digital reference and the internship may be too brief for these skills to be acquired, but some experience with the various forms of reference provision will at least help the student understand the different interview skills and resources that are essential to these services. Knowledge of the reference interview and resources is a vital part of the reference internship. Whether the experience is designed to include a special project, a variety of tasks, or a concentration on public desk work, the structure must be established before the intern arrives so that there is no question about the work to be accomplished.

Provide adequate space and equipment for the intern. If possible the intern should have a desk, preferably with a computer. This helps emphasize the intern's transition from student to professional and provides a place where work may be organized. A space of one's own affords a "retreat" where the student can reflect on lessons learned and/or regroup if client interaction seems overwhelming. Although providing a separate desk may be impossible for many institutions, the lack of space and equipment need not prevent the library from offering internships. Indeed, young librarians may confront similar difficulties in their first professional job. An enthusiastic and supportive reference staff can compensate for what the physical environment may lack.

Establish a supportive work environment. Interns need to ask questions—lots of questions. They may think that asking too many questions or displaying ignorance creates a bad impression; they must, therefore, be made to feel comfortable in these situations. Staff's role in the training process is to successfully integrate the intern into the total culture of the reference department, including collegial information sharing.

A good orientation prepares the intern and the reference department for a successful partnership. The orientation may take more than one day, depending on the intern's schedule and the size of the reference department. The orientation should include:

Meeting with the internship coordinator to review the schedule, objectives of the internship, and the intern training manual. An overview of proposed projects, usually appropriate at this time, may be equally appropriate after the intern is settled.

A tour of the library and all its departments, with introductions to staff.

Assigning the intern's desk space.

Informing the intern how to acquire supplies, use the library's computer network and e-mail, register for a library card, etc.

Reviewing the reference department staff manual.

Meeting with all reference staff, preferably during an hour when staff have time to explain their specific jobs to the intern.

Observing at the reference desk. The librarian should meet with the intern beforehand and then go to the desk together for observation and instruction.

Introducing the intern to print and nonprint resources, providing special instruction for library electronic resources.

Discussing and preparing the project. If special supplies or equipment are required, confirm that they will be obtained.

The schedule will depend on the number of hours required by the educational institution and the intern's school or work schedule. Ideally the schedule will include one or two weekdays and one weekend day. This allows the intern to experience the different types of clientele who may visit the reference desk throughout the week. Initially, internship hours should be scheduled for the least busy reference desk times so the student and staff can develop better rapport when not dealing with a heavy client load. Scheduling interns during slow times will also enable them to learn departmental resources and procedures and develop confidence. The schedule may be shifted to busier hours as the intern gains skill and sufficient self-confidence. A fast-paced reference desk helps one develop the ability to think quickly and to manage client load. It may also help create a "can do" attitude and a sense of belonging—of really contributing to the work of the department.

Do not schedule the intern alone on the reference desk. Reference staff should teach professional skills and techniques and not expect the intern to simply pick them up from experience. Neither the department, the student, nor the clients are well served by expecting too much from the intern.

If possible, get the intern to commit to working at least two school terms (approximately six months). Less time makes assigning projects problematic and provides minimal direct public desk and teaching experience. Interns who already have reference desk exposure may profit from shorter training periods, but it is essential for those with little experience to have the maximum time available.

The internship training manual and the reference department staff manual should teach reference procedures, delineate best practices, define objectives, and offer review and self-evaluation instruments for the intern's use. In addition, the internship manual should include:

> information on the library and the reference department: library mission, organization charts, the work of the reference department, staffing configurations, expected reference competencies;
> information on the reference interview: articles, tips, self-evaluation protocols;
> a checklist of reference skills: knowledge of print and nonprint resources, knowledge of department equipment (computers, copy machines, microform readers, etc.);
> a self-test on library resources; and
> an orientation checklist: were all facets of the orientation completed?

REFERENCE DESK TRAINING

The most important aspect of the internship is training at the reference desk itself. Interns who have little or no experience at the reference desk will learn to apply theory to practice, develop communication skills, gain knowledge of a wide range of resources, and, if the internship is successful, decide that reference librarianship is the appropriate career choice. Interns with some experience will sharpen their skills and may acquire knowledge about telephone and virtual reference.

Provide the intern plenty of opportunity to practice the reference interview in a variety of reference settings: the reference desk, telephone reference, and virtual reference. Pair the intern with different reference librarians to permit him or her to observe a variety of interview styles and techniques. Offer positive suggestions for improving techniques and avoid dominating the reference interview. Counsel reference staff to be a supportive presence at the reference desk and to offer constructive criticism in private. Experienced reference librarians often find it difficult to keep silent when the interview is not going smoothly; but interns need to build confidence and proficiency. Interruptions should be limited unless it really is necessary to step in.

Always explain "why." At the reference desk try to explain why an interview is conducted in a certain way, why one resource is selected over another, and why the service should be tailored to fit the client. Explain why the intern might want to locate and print a magazine article for an elderly woman rather than directing her to the library's computers; why the ten-year-old with an economics assignment is helped at the reference desk rather than being sent to the children's department; why the library's remote access resources are always suggested to clients; why copyright notices are included on materials faxed to clients; why some resources are recommended only in electronic format; and why referrals are provided. "Why" is a vital part of the learning process. Do not hesitate to point out how an experienced librarian's interview might have been improved. Explain what other questions might have been asked to elicit the client's needs or what better resources could have been recommended. Professional reference librarians do occasionally have lapses in judgment, and these may be used as learning opportunities. By critiquing their own interview skills, reference librarians show the intern that learning is continuous, thus helping to lessen the student's anxiety about mistakes.

Interns with little experience will probably spend most of their time on the reference desk, developing basic interviewing skills and matching information needs with appropriate resources. Given the relatively short duration of an internship, the reference desk should be a priority for studying techniques and learning to deal with the public.

While inexperienced interns may be allowed to observe alternative forms of reference service, experienced interns should be given the opportunity to develop skills in telephone and virtual reference. Not only will these students be able to enhance their skills, but future employers will benefit as well.

Introducing the intern to print resources is imperative. Currently, much course emphasis is placed on electronic databases and Internet sites, sometimes to the detriment of standard print resources. Interns will learn that even in the most well-equipped library the best resource to answer a question may be the telephone directory—a valuable lesson that is less likely to be taught in library school. Developing the ability to assess the client's information need and match it to the appropriate resource—print or electronic—is a skill reference librarians must be equipped to provide.

Equally important is the reference librarian's demeanor. Help the intern focus on the client first. Watch the intern's interaction with the client and discuss it afterward. An observer's checklist, similar to those used by library school students doing observation, helps. Despite the lessons learned when observing unreceptive reference librarians, the students may, when faced with real clients, exhibit the very same behaviors. Based on real-life reference observations, construct a checklist (see appendix 7A) to be used in observing the intern. Such a checklist gives credibility to the observations and may help soften the critique.

DEVELOPING INTERNSHIP PROJECTS

Establish a specific project or a set of activities that will be of value to both the library and the intern. Although you may prefer that the project be completed by the end of the internship, working on a discrete part of a larger project may also be rewarding. Because students sometimes have rather grand ideas for projects based on their assigned readings, staff may have to balance enthusiasm with departmental needs. Never accept a proposed project that is unrealistic in terms of time, resources, or needs.

Projects should fit within established departmental programs. For instance, the intern might be asked to design a bibliographic instruction class as part of a series and then conduct that class to complete the project. He or she might also be asked to research materials for a subject bibliography or take on collection development tasks. Some interns enjoy sorting and distributing gift books to the subject selectors, following the process through until the books are on the shelves. Other possible projects include: developing searchable question archives/knowledge bases; developing virtual library tours; designing library Web pages; and designing browsing and searching aids that facilitate unmediated services.

EVALUATING INTERN PERFORMANCE

Intern evaluations may take several forms. First, the library school will no doubt provide formal evaluation guidelines, including assessment of:

> application of theory to practice;
> learning ability;
> working effectively with staff;
> dealing effectively with clients;
> quality and quantity of work;
> communication skills;
> appearance; and
> positive qualities or reservations.

Be honest in these evaluations. Discussing the evaluation with the faculty advisor gives the intern an opportunity to profit from your observations. Meeting frequently with the student during the internship improves the chance of a good final evaluation.

The reference department may also wish to have its own evaluation that focuses on specific skills acquired during the internship. Such an evaluation may take the form of a self-test that the intern uses to measure proficiency and the need for additional training. Furthermore, interns may provide valuable feedback by evaluating the reference department. Students should be asked how the internship was particularly effective as well as how the process might be improved. The intern's evaluation of the experience may assess:

opportunities to set and achieve goals and objectives;
availability of reference staff for training and consultation;
training on reference policies and procedures;
an assigned project or specific tasks that were completed;
interaction with all reference staff;
observation of various interview and search techniques;
training in and observation of all reference activities; and
receiving frequent feedback on progress and projects.

The formal evaluation, the reference department evaluation, and the intern's own evaluation are tools to be used to develop a successful internship program.

APPENDIX 7A

Sample Checklist of Reference Desk Skills

1. Reference interview, performance standards, resource review
   ❑ satisfactory   ❑ needs work
2. Searching the online catalog by author, title, subject, keyword, call number
   ❑ satisfactory   ❑ needs work
3. Knowledge of reference desk ready reference collection
   ❑ satisfactory   ❑ needs work
4. Using electronic databases resources
   ❑ satisfactory   ❑ needs work
5. Instructing clients in the use of library database products
   ❑ satisfactory   ❑ needs work
6. Searching the Internet to retrieve information
   ❑ satisfactory   ❑ needs work
7. Instructing clients in the use of the Internet to retrieve information
   ❑ satisfactory   ❑ needs work
8. Knowledge of reference subject collections:
   Business   ❑ satisfactory   ❑ needs work
   Law   ❑ satisfactory   ❑ needs work
   Foundation/Grants ❑ satisfactory   ❑ needs work

• *8* •

"And Other Duties as Assigned": Iowa City Public Library's First Children's Services Intern

Denise H. Britigan

$\mathscr{T}$he advertisement came across the University of Iowa School of Library and Information Science (SLIS) electronic discussion list in July:

> The Iowa City Public Library is looking for a SLIS student who is interested in an internship in Children's Services. September 2001 to August 2002; 10 hrs./wk during the academic year; 40 hrs./wk in the summer; $8.00/hour. Requirements: SLIS Student. Knowledge of children's literature. For details, see the SLIS Job Book in the office or contact the library directly.

I printed it out and thought it over. I was always looking for skills to add to my professional toolkit and this looked intriguing. But at the same time, I wasn't sure I could juggle raising my two teenagers, attending graduate school full-time, fulfilling my commitments to the organizations to which I belonged, and handling an internship, too. Since I was enrolled in the summer cataloging course, I sought out the advice of my instructor, Greg Cotton. He said that it is easy to get "pigeonholed" in this profession and that I should experience what it is like to work in a public library while I had the opportunity. He also wisely added, "Besides, if you don't even apply, you'll always wonder, 'What if . . . ?'"

So I did apply. I was soon invited to interview for the position. By the end of the interview, I was offered the job. It was decided that I would begin on September 10. My time and energy were to be divided equally between the children's services area and a statewide literacy initiative called "Christie Vilsack's Stories 2000." The children's services (CS) portion would be supervised by the CS coordinator, Debb Green, and the "Stories 2000" portion would be supervised by the then–assistant director of the library, Elizabeth Nichols. I was to be their very first intern.

73

IOWA CITY PUBLIC LIBRARY

With a population of 62, 220, Iowa City is the sixth largest city in the state of Iowa. The Iowa City Public Library (ICPL) serves its city residents as well as residents of the surrounding unincorporated Johnson County. The library's collection contains over 210,000 items and circulation tops 1.3 million a year. Sixty people work at the library. The children's services area itself has three librarians, one of whom is full-time (the coordinator), and four library assistants, all of whom have college degrees and some children's literature and programming expertise. During my internship, ICPL was in the throes of a massive expansion project. The children's services area alone increased from 4,400 to 10,200 square feet.

My orientation to children's services included a tour of the area, a verbal description of each part of the collection and which librarian was responsible for what, policies, and a schedule of meetings that I was expected to attend. I was to be involved in the following projects: collection management and development, supplies storage, video archives, various story times, the winter break program, the Children's Day/Arts Festival, and the summer reading program, along with "other duties as assigned." For Stories 2000, I was expected to enter current data into a database, analyze the data to determine reading program gaps, take minutes at meetings with other librarians in Johnson County, organize book discussion groups, and find venues for new reading program opportunities.

COLLECTION MANAGEMENT AND DEVELOPMENT

In preparation for the expansion and impending move into temporarily smaller space, I was involved in some weeding and collection development practices. This was a very hands-on application of what I had learned in my collection development course in the SLIS program. One of my responsibilities in this area was to use a computer printout to pull children's picture books that had circulated more than a hundred times. The books were then evaluated by the CS coordinator to determine if they should be discarded, replaced, or returned to the circulating collection. Since the library was involved in a huge expansion project that would limit space before the new larger CS area would open in spring 2004, the books were scrutinized carefully. If a replacement copy was needed, I determined availability and cost from a variety of vendors. I compiled a spreadsheet for this purpose.

Another project involved verifying staff booklists against actual holdings. I was asked to determine the number of copies that ICPL had in the current collection for each title. These lists were eventually edited if the books were no longer in circulation and no longer in print. Similarly, I was asked to check the online catalog for holdings of new materials based on review journals for the jE, jFiction, and jNonfiction collections. The librarians in charge of those collections would then order materials as needed. I also had the privilege of working on updating a booklist that was based on an order list by Hazel Westgate, former CS coordinator and longtime librarian at the ICPL. The booklist was made available as a brochure for patrons.

In addition, I tackled the craft supplies collection cupboard. I used uniform, clear plastic bins to sort, inventory, and label a wide variety of supplies. This made it possible for the librarians to use what was available to them in a more efficient manner. It may not sound like a very important task, but it proved to be one with a very visible impact and was much appreciated by the staff.

STORY TIMES AND CHILDREN'S PROGRAMMING

Although I had not taken any courses to prepare me to work in the children's area, I had lived the role expected of me. By being a mother of youngsters who loved the public library, I saw firsthand what a difference the ICPL children's services staff and programming made in my children's lives. I sought out the opportunity to emulate the people who had so impressed me over the years, consistently providing quality resources and service to the Iowa City community.

Although I had some initial anxiety about story times and children's programming, they turned out to be among my favorite experiences. I actually looked forward to the challenges that each one presented! I was asked to conduct an occasional family story time on Saturday mornings, toddler story times on Tuesday mornings, and preschool story times on Thursday mornings. Preparation for story times included the selection of a theme (optional), the selection of appropriate program materials (books, finger plays, handouts, or short video), setting the stage (props and visual aids), and the reading aloud of books. These performances were sometimes videotaped for simulcast on public access television (Channel 10) and also saved as a videotape for future broadcasting on the the library channel. It was important to provide the copyright information for any materials used during a taped program. This information was given to the audiovisual services desk with the VHS tape so that public performance permission could be obtained for the library. Friends still occasionally mention that they've recently seen me on TV because the tapes are rerun periodically.

I also assisted with special Thursday afternoon Kids Spectacular performance events, coordinated by the librarian who regularly worked with older elementary and junior high school students. This entailed tackling various logis-
tical tasks, including helping with set design (for example, a dragon's cave or a
unicorn's cart) and managing crowd control. We had hundreds of families attend these popular free events.

As any children's services staff person can tell you, the summer reading
program is a big deal. I worked forty hours a week for the months of June, July,
and part of August. Aspects of my job included preparing hundreds of "prize
bags" (containing a certificate of completion, free giveaways, coupons, or mis-
cellaneous theme-related material), enrolling the participants (by explaining
the program verbally and helping them manually register), and giving guidance
to participants as they made their way through the check-box lists of required
readings. There were various lists for various reading levels. My voice gave out
on me more than once after eight hours of recruitment in a day. That summer,
we had over 1,400 children register to participate.

JOHNSON COUNTY STORIES 2000: "TELLING OUR STORIES"

The current First Lady of Iowa, Christie Vilsack, is a librarian. She believes in
a statewide "stories program" and so started the "Stories 2000" movement.
Since then, at least fifty community libraries across Iowa have become participants. The idea was to create a network of reading programs within each
county. By identifying the literacy efforts promoted by various volunteer organizations and agencies throughout the county, the program could identify
gap areas. This led to a collaboration to coordinate efforts and expand practices. Librarians met with teachers, media specialists, members of philanthropic
organizations, civic program leaders, and volunteers to poll information about
what already exists and what could become reality in the future.

In general, for this project, my role as an intern involved being an aide to
Elizabeth Nichols, the then–assistant director of the Iowa City Public Library.
This included doing a variety of jobs as needed, such as attending advisory
board meetings, attending implementation team meetings, typing up and distributing minutes from the meetings, creating a database of the agencies' reading programs in the Johnson County area, telephoning and e-mailing organizations for funding support and/or participation, and making presentations
before interested businesses and/or organizations. Currently, sixty-five local
agencies oversee 164 literacy projects in Johnson County. I continued to be involved in this project post-internship as my schedule permitted.

REFLECTIONS

Time management was probably my biggest challenge during the internship. Not only was there a balance of Stories 2000 (five hours/week) and children's services (five hours/week), but some follow-up work was done at home as well. In addition, I still needed to fulfill my graduation requirements while I was involved in the internship. This meant completing my course requirements (including a practicum elsewhere) and taking my written and oral comprehensive exams during the spring semester. I was successful in this endeavor and graduated with a master's degree in May 2002, three months before the internship was completed.

Although the library staff were extremely supportive, answering my questions and instructing me in their techniques, I often felt pulled in many directions. I suggest that, as much as possible, the intern be apprised of programming duties/expectations in writing ahead of time. Communication is always appreciated and improves the end result for all concerned. For example, in hindsight, had I known in advance what I learned from reviewing a taped story time with a librarian, my own first story time would have been better. I appreciated constructive criticism and tried to incorporate what I learned into what I did.

I am grateful to have been the first intern at ICPL and encourage all library school students to participate in a children's services internship if they want to get a good idea of what it's like to work in a public library. Although the salary may seem low ($8 an hour), the benefits of having the opportunity to gain experience far outweigh the rate of pay. I did not know at the time of my internship what library position my future would hold, since I consider myself more of a generalist, with a health science background, than a children's librarian.

In addition, my experience taught the Iowa City Public Library what it was like to have an intern. As Debb Green has said, it was a win-win scenario for both the library and me. Being an intern gives one the opportunity to constantly learn about something new. The knowledge one gains can't be read in a book—you can't anticipate all the jobs you may be asked to do, nor can you predict the impact that it will have on your future. Internships provide the opportunity to add new skills to your basket. I apply many of the skills I learned in my internship to my job today. I learned to smile at people in front of me to put them at ease when they ask me a question. I learned that it is important to be open-minded to the wide variety of books that a child, teenager, or adult wishes to read. I learned that parents appreciate guidance. I learned that children's librarians are very willing to share knowledge. Finally, I learned that the Iowa City Public Library interns that have come after me have all been unique. And that ICPL has loved each and every one of us.

How I Spent My Summer Vacation:
An Internship Experience at
New York Public Library's Teen Central

Erica Tang

*W*hen the New York Public Library's Nathan Straus Branch for Children and Young People first opened in 1941, only patrons under the age of twenty-one were allowed to borrow books from its collection. Located on East 32nd Street, the branch flourished through the early 1950s as something of a "laboratory" where staff could experiment with new collection materials and innovative programs. Although it functioned successfully as a neighborhood library, Nathan Straus also attracted young people from all around the city and served as a training ground for new librarians specializing in youth services.

In 1953, the branch closed and a majority of its collection moved to the mezzanine floor of the Donnell Library on 53rd Street, where it has been housed ever since. Fifty years later, the space was renovated and reopened as Nathan Straus Teen Central. With approximately 28,000 books, seventy magazines, its own CD and DVD collection, and twelve computer stations, Teen Central is dedicated to serving teens ages twelve to eighteen and grades seven through twelve.

CONSIDERING MY OPTIONS

As a first-year master's student at the UCLA Department of Information Studies, I began thinking about gaining field experience early on. I knew I wanted some experience working at a public library—specifically with youth—and that an internship would be the perfect way to do this. Since the UCLA program requires students to fulfill a minimum of thirty-six units (nine classes) before applying for an internship, the earliest I could complete one was the summer after my first year. As eager as I was to get started, I realized summer was a good time not only to explore opportunities in my area, but also perhaps to apply for internships on the East Coast, where I grew up and where my immediate family still lives. An internship in New York would allow me to spend time with my family, as well as gain the experience I wanted from a public library.

The New York Public Library (NYPL), with its rich history and prestige in the library world, seemed like an ideal place to intern. Having grown up in New Jersey, I have always loved everything about New York City—its energy, its complexity, and its diversity. Since I was particularly interested in teens, I decided to research young adult (YA) services at NYPL. I found information about the current Nathan Straus Teen Central on the library's website. I further researched and read about some of its innovative programs and publications, including *Books for the Teen Age*—a comprehensive booklet listing new and favorite books for teens by genre and subject matter. I was impressed with the information I found about Teen Central and decided to try to arrange an internship there.

I called Teen Central directly and asked to speak to a supervisor. I was then connected to the supervising librarian, Joanne, who seemed enthusiastic at the idea of having an intern, since her division never had one before. She also explained that the library was revamping and remodeling Teen Central and that it would reopen in February. We arranged a day to meet in December, when I would be on the East Coast visiting my family for the holidays. I was on my way.

THE SETUP

In December, I met with Joanne and took a short tour of Teen Central. I was impressed by the space and the amount of materials the library owned. Joanne explained that their collection catered to the community they served—over one million teenagers in all three boroughs (Manhattan, Staten Island, and the Bronx) served by NYPL. This made Teen Central a unique facility and justified the volume of materials. The space was still undergoing renovation, so everything was new and untouched. Located on the mezzanine of the Donnell Library, Teen Central was separated from the rest of the floor—which was mainly dedicated to reference services and administrative offices—by soundproof glass.

There were rows and rows of teen fiction, nonfiction, and classics, as well as tall, clear plastic shelves that showcased YA titles—from award-winning literature to "staff picks." The space also featured computer stations, a big flat-screen TV with its own lounge area, some circular study tables, a larger rectangular table for teen advisory board meetings and other programs, and a corner area filled with DVDs, CDs, and audio books. Joanne explained that once Teen Central reopened, only teens would be allowed in this area. Although children and adults were allowed to browse, they would not be able to sit and remain at the tables.

With a project already in mind, Joanne showed me the quiet study room, which was part of Teen Central but was enclosed in glass for students who wanted a quieter environment. Within this room was another collection of books, called the Historical Young Adult Collection. This collection contained books from the original Nathan Straus Library, as well as items that had been pulled off the library's circulation shelves. For various reasons, librarians felt that certain titles and authors were too "significant" to discard and so moved them into the historical collection instead.

This mixture of books filled about eight shelves. About two-thirds of the titles were fiction, while the rest were nonfiction. Joanne believed that this collection could be developed into a significant research tool for students, scholars, and librarians. A unique collection like this, where significant young adult literature existed all in one place, could be used by all types of people interested in the historical aspects of YA literature. Helping develop such a valuable collection would no doubt be a challenging project, but one that I felt I could learn a lot from and could make great contributions to. Joanne said if I was interested, she'd love to have me as an intern. Once she knew that I was sure I wanted to do it, she would contact Human Resources.

When I returned to Los Angeles, I met with my advisor, Cindy, to share my thoughts about this possible internship. I told her about the collection development idea, as well as the opportunity to work in this newly remodeled center. Since I had not taken the collection development course yet, I knew I needed some guidance from both her and the librarians I would be working with at NYPL. Initially I was a bit unsure about whether I could produce quality results without first taking the appropriate course work. But Joanne did not mind my lack of class experience and assured me that we would work together to analyze the collection and develop a management policy.

Cindy, who also teaches the collection development course at UCLA, devised three assignments for me to follow throughout the internship: (1) evaluating the collection; (2) developing a collection statement/policy; and (3) selecting materials for the collection. The first assignment was designed to help me assess the existing collection—from its physical materials to the factors that influence development of the collection, to the budget and additional considerations for maintaining the collection. After an in-depth analysis of the collection, the second assignment directed me in drafting a collection development statement, using the information and analysis from assignment number one. The third assignment built on the second and used the written collection development statement as a guideline for selecting new materials to strengthen the collection. Although I would not be able to produce polished papers for each, I knew that these assignments would help me keep a steady work pace throughout the internship. Through e-mail, I would check in with Cindy on a regular basis, show her my work along the way, and get her feedback.

With my advisor's approval, I contacted Joanne to confirm my internship, and we agreed on start and end dates. The full internship would last about six weeks—not much time, but realistically I could stay for only a short period before my funds would begin to run out. Accomplishing everything in six weeks would be challenging; I therefore decided that the best way to get the most out of this internship was to work full-time.

In the meantime, Joanne sent a summary of the proposed internship project to Human Resources. I was to review the existing collection, identify gaps through a survey of important titles in YA literature, and produce both a recommended list of additions and deletions to the collection and a written collection development policy. By April, my summer internship at NYPL was set. I couldn't wait to start.

FIRST IMPRESSIONS

My first few days in New York were a bit of a whirlwind. I spent the first part of the morning of my first day at NYPL's Human Resources department, which was located in another library in midtown Manhattan. Once there, I filled out some paperwork and verified my position as an intern and my location at the Donnell Library's Nathan Straus Teen Central. I was given a booklet on policies and a brief orientation. NYPL has both paid and unpaid interns, but it does not have a formal internship program. Instead, interns are chosen on a case-by-case basis, with the individual departments deciding whether or not the interns will be paid. Although I was not getting paid, I nonetheless felt the experience would be worthwhile.

Joanne spent the first day showing me around the Donnell Library and introducing me to other librarians and library workers. After reassessing the project goals, we created a timeline for completing the project. I also helped her prepare for opening Teen Central by turning on the computers, logging into the network, and straightening up the area. Once the library was open, Joanne turned on all the lights, as well as the stereo and surround-sound system. The CD changer was filled with a variety of music genres, from hip hop to rock to rhythm and blues to alternative, and the stereo played all day long.

It was a different environment from other teen spaces I had visited. The music seemed to welcome the teenagers to stay a while.

Teen Central is certainly a unique place, one that encourages young people to sit and "hang out." Although patrons of all ages can browse the shelves and walk around the area, no adults—unless they are accompanying a teen—or children—unless accompanied by a teen—are allowed to stay. The only exception is the quiet study room, which houses the historical collection. The "no adult" rule was a factor to consider as I analyzed and worked on the main focus of my internship, the collection development project.

THE PROJECT

Joanne wanted to see two main products at the end of the project: a written collection development policy and a list of suggested titles for the collection, using the criteria set forth in the policy. She explained that she wanted me to list as many titles as possible because, although they did not have the funds right then to acquire all the items, they might be able to obtain more funds and books in the future. A large portion of the policy was to address retrospective development—titles that would fill the gaps in the already existing collection. Books that did not belong in the collection would need to be weeded, since there was limited space for adding new materials.

I was also to consider that the historical collection did not have an allocated budget. The librarians, therefore, needed to find "creative" ways of obtaining titles that they did not already own—everything from pulling books from existing collections to shifting budget money allocated to other areas. Joanne eventually hoped to provide enough justification for the historical collection to have its own budget. She believed writing a policy and reorganizing the collection were a good place to start.

By the end of the day, Joanne handed me an inventory of all the titles supposedly located in the quiet study room. My first task was to cross-check the list with the actual books on the shelves. This would get me familiar with the titles and the types of books already in the collection. I also read through existing NYPL collection development and materials policies to get an idea of the library's service community and collections. I spoke to the two other full-time YA librarians at Teen Central and asked them questions about the historical collection. They stressed that the books weren't used very often, but occasionally someone from the publishing or media industries visited the collection to research youth culture, both past and present. Also, adults sometimes stopped by, browsed the titles, and reminisced. I remember one woman who visited the quiet study room to browse the collection because she was looking for particular titles by an author she loved as a teenager. Nathan Straus was the only place that owned these books. She spent some time flipping through the pages of different novels and rereading some of the stories.

While evaluating the collection, I found some fascinating older books published around or before the 1940s that bore the original Nathan Straus library address stamp. Some were even stamped with circulation dates as early as 1941. Several were so yellowed and brittle that I was afraid further examination would cause the book to fall apart. I pulled those books that seemed especially fragile to show to Joanne. I also made a note of the publication years of all the books, in case we needed to consider copyright as part of the policy's retention criteria.

After reviewing the seven-hundred-plus titles in the fiction section, I found no real patterns in the way the books were collected. The books fell into two major categories: old books from the original Nathan Straus branch—with no indication of whether certain books were kept for specific purposes or whether they represent "whatever was left" after the library's move into Donnell—and more contemporary books that *may* be considered historically significant and, therefore, were pulled off the shelves and saved from being discarded. Without a previous collection development policy, it is possible that past and present librarians used their own definitions of "historical significance" to place books in this collection—definitions that widely varied according to the opinions of the librarians. Providing a broad but clear definition of "historical significance" in the realm of young adult literature was a major task I considered when writing the collection development policy.

It took me over a week to cross-check the fiction titles. In addition, I reviewed several resources to get an idea of what experts believe are "quality" and "representative" young adult literature. Among the titles I surveyed were *Literature for Today's Young Adults* by Aileen Pace Nilsen and Kenneth L. Donnelson (Scott, Foresman, 1989), *From Romance to Realism: 50 Years of Growth and Change in Young Adult Literature* by Michael Cart (HarperCollins, 1996), and various booklists, such as the Michael Printz Award and the American Library Association's *Best Books for Young Adults* lists.

I also visited the children's historical collection, which is located one floor above Teen Central. I met with John, who was then the senior librarian in the central children's room at Donnell, and talked to him about the children's historical collection. Basically I wanted to know how librarians determine what belongs in the historical collection, in terms of a book's *quality* and *significance*. John reminded me that before becoming part of NYPL's collection, all books must undergo a stringent "passing" process and so are already considered to uphold a certain quality. However, in order to be part of the historical collection, a title needs to be recommended by a librarian. These books then go through a second "passing" process for approval into the historical collection. Although there is no written policy for the children's historical collection, most suggestions are made by seasoned children's librarians who understand the materials and their multiple purposes as historical artifacts.

After a week, Joanne and I met to discuss the work I had done so far. We agreed that I should concentrate on the fiction section of the collection, since nonfiction would probably require a different policy. We also created a broad definition of historically significant young adult literature, which I included in the policy as:

> Historical significance, as it is defined within this policy, broadly includes— but is not limited to—authors and works that have made major contributions to the field of young adult literature. These selected works possess qualities that stand out from general young adult fiction, such as "breakthrough" themes and styles and award-winning status.

Although this is a rather broad statement, we felt it provided some criteria for choosing titles in the future. I also added a statement that basically explains that, when making final decisions, the librarian in charge of the collection will provide guidance in the weeding and maintenance of the materials. Like the "second passing process" of the children's historical collection, seasoned YA librarians who know the literature would make such decisions.

Using the *Collection Development and Resources Access Plan for the Skokie Public Library* (distributed by the Public Library Association, 1998) as a template, I began writing the collection development statement. I included the research and information gathered on the target community, the overall collection description, and influencing factors—such as the limited space and the lack of budget. I constructed selection and retention and weeding plans, naming important resources and award-winning lists as guides, as well as a development plan, which envisioned the future direction of the collection.

Once I wrote the policy, I applied my selection plan to the collection itself. I compiled a long bibliography of award-winning titles and renowned authors of young adult literature. Titles were repeated if they received more than one award or were mentioned in more than one source—a feature that may be helpful in establishing priorities for obtaining the most notable books.

After constructing this list, I then highlighted any title that already existed in the current historical collection. In addition, Joanne suggested that I explore the remnants of their young adult circuit collection (CNY), which contains books that are used to supplement branch collections. Librarians could borrow books out of the CNY collection for four months at a time. These books were used to enhance the collection for class visits and special projects. Because NYPL had stopped buying CNY books, the collection—which librarians no longer use—was being phased out. I spent a few days scouring through the collection and pulled out a good number of books that were on my selection list.

Although I accomplished quite a lot, I did not have time to do several things: (1) I was unable to properly weed the collection in order to make room for the books I had gathered; (2) I was unable to further examine the selection list with the other librarians and establish a priority for the titles; and (3) I was unable to discuss with Joanne some ideas for revitalizing interest in the historical collection in order to justify its own budget. However, during my six-week internship at NYPL, I did create tools and products for Joanne and Teen Central to utilize, and hopefully improve upon, in the future.

WRAPPING IT UP

This internship taught me the importance, and necessity, of taking initiative. By defining my goals early on and exploring my possibilities, I was able to obtain an internship that afforded me invaluable experience, both in collection development and young adult services. It was a unique experience for me because I had not taken a collection development course and so used the guidance of several professionals, as well as my instincts and my desire to learn, as fuel for writing and developing a policy that is both practical and visionary. Collection development and research made up the majority of my internship experience.

I also spent time observing, learning, and generally helping at Teen Central. I worked with librarians and teen workers at the reference desk, helping parents and young people find books, answering simple questions about the library and the library catalog, and monitoring computer use. I helped process new CDs and DVDs and talked to teen volunteers. I observed and participated in programs—from teen advisory board meetings to movie screenings to author programs to class visits. I even visited a high school and observed the way different librarians administered book talks and information sessions for summer school classes. I was also extremely fortunate to work with several encouraging librarians who were more than happy to mentor me and talk about their interests and involvement as YA librarians. I received advice on joining discussion lists, working with teens, getting current with YA literature, and doing book talks.

Perhaps one of my most memorable and insightful experiences was talking to teenagers on a daily basis. The "regular" visitors were open, intelligent, energetic, and eager to share things about themselves. I admired their honesty and, as the weeks went by, grew more comfortable talking and working with them. I also received great advice from them—about books, movies, and certain trends. Mostly, I gained a better understanding of what makes a space like Teen Central feel safe and secure.

This idea of comfort and security resonated during one particular program. The teens had a party to celebrate the publication and distribution of their 'zine, "Unlimited." As a result of writing workshops that took place during the previous spring, teens expressed their ideas and emotions through stories, poetry, and drawings, which they then shared at the 'zine party. What I heard was amazing—the poems and stories, the jokes and descriptions, the intelligent musings, and the constant (but playful) battling for the microphone. It was a wonderful program and I loved hearing the eagerness and confidence in their voices. It made such a great impression on me, and it remains one of my most memorable moments at Teen Central.

My internship at NYPL was filled with rich and invaluable experiences. I gained more confidence working with the public, especially teenagers, and became familiar with the ideals and practices of an institution known for producing pioneers in youth services. As an intern, I felt I was treated like an equal at Teen Central. I worked on a genuinely challenging project and received constant guidance and thoughtful advice. My supervisor, Joanne, and the other YA librarians were true mentors during my stay at NYPL. I will always appreciate their patience and attentiveness to my questions and suggestions. Overall, I believe that creating a positive internship experience means setting realistic goals and initiatives, communicating effectively and regularly, and possessing an open mind.

Many people say this about the internship experience: "It is what you make of it." I couldn't agree more. What I made out of this six-week internship—the people I met, the work I did, the lessons I learned—will remain with me throughout my career.

LEEPing into the Profession:
Interning at the Vacaville Public Library

Michelle Ornat and Linda Matchette

$\mathcal{T}$he opportunity to do an internship can manifest itself in both usual and unusual ways. When Michelle walked into the Vacaville (California) Public Library to assess its young adult area for a school project focused on designing a space for teens, she didn't know she'd walk out with an interview date for an internship. With her attention elsewhere, she hadn't imagined she'd be doing any real networking. In the course of an hour, she had managed to round out ideas for her teen space project and set herself on track for an internship in her final semester of graduate school.

THE GUMPTION TO ASK

After a preliminary survey of the teen area and the collection, Michelle met with the young adult librarian, Molly, to talk about the philosophy of Vacaville's teen space and its services to kids. During the conversation, Molly mentioned she was a UCLA graduate and that her position as young adult librarian was her first professional job. She had enjoyed the program at UCLA, but felt she should have done an internship before applying for positions. An internship would have given her more practical experience and an idea about the workings of a public library. Michelle agreed. Her own need to intern had become more obvious as graduation approached; she needed real library experience.

After having applied for some paraprofessional library jobs and being unsuccessful in getting anything other than volunteer work, Michelle feared she wouldn't be able to land a professional position upon graduation. When Molly suggested that she seriously pursue an internship, Michelle took that advice to heart and asked in the next sentence whether there would be a possibility to intern right there at the Vacaville Public Library. That afternoon, Molly introduced Michelle to Linda, the supervising librarian, and a date was set for an interview. With a seemingly routine visit to the library, the unexpected encouragement and openness of a peer, a little gumption to ask the question, and the willingness of a potential mentor, the wheels were set in motion for an internship.

During the next meeting, Linda and Michelle each presented their needs and expectations. Michelle clearly needed the chance to gain experience working in a library. Linda had herself been a library trainee at the Tompkins County Public Library in Ithaca, New York, and saw that these opportunities were mutually beneficial. She understood that Michelle would get some good public library experience, while at the same time helping out with collection development.

GAINING PRACTICAL EXPERIENCE

When Michelle began her internship at the Vacaville branch of the Solano County Library, she was a master's student in LEEP, the online distance learning program of the Graduate School of Library and Information Science (GSLIS) at the University of Illinois, Urbana–Champaign. In her final semester, she enrolled in GSLIS's practicum course. It was the perfect option for a student like Michelle who did not have any practical library experience and lived two thousand miles away from campus. The practicum provided an opportunity for students to work in libraries when they couldn't participate in campus-based student work programs or university-funded positions. A practicum-based internship was an opportune way to secure professional-level library experience without having to apply for work or wait to finish the master's degree.

Having been previously undecided about what type of library career to follow, Michelle drew on her interests, both personal and academic, in public libraries. The basic requirements for completion of the internship were: a practicum résumé; coordination of the practicum with the GSLIS practicum coordinator, the practicum faculty advisor and the site supervisor, Linda; negotiation and creation of a practicum contract or individualized educational plan; submission of a practicum project abstract; and completion of one hundred hours of fieldwork experience with no more than 25 percent of that time devoted to a special project.

The goal of the internship was for Michelle to gain experience through both performing and observing professional-level duties. Linda printed up monthly schedules, consulted with Michelle on days and hours when she would be available, and started lining up staff for her to spend time with. Scheduling was relatively easy since Michelle had no other class or job conflicts to work around. Being available mostly in the mornings, she was able to attend meetings and take advantage of "closed" time to communicate with others on observations and any other questions that came up.

Linda integrated both the theoretical and the practical aspects of librarianship when she designed Michelle's internship plan. Because the library is organized with one information desk, Michelle became acquainted with staff who offered services to children and teens as well as adults. When not on the desk, she was encouraged to spend time familiarizing herself with the collection. She browsed and learned how to use the catalog to search for materials. She also became familiar with the SNAP (Solano Napa and Partners) consortium's circulation system so she could place holds for patrons.

Linda and Michelle reviewed organizational hierarchies and budgets and discussed the library's policies and procedures, paying particular attention to the collection development policy. Since her practicum coincided with the next year's planning phase, she was able to observe the process of reviewing standing orders and collection development plans for the following fiscal year. The county's budgets, which are somewhat complex, were explained in detail.

Through meetings and conversations, Michelle learned about the mission of the Vacaville Public Library, its goals and objectives, the community it serves, and the library consortium to which it belongs. From the managers, she learned about the philosophy of library administration and resource allocation. At staff meetings, she observed, firsthand, the effects of technology on staff, gained insight into the division of labor between management and library departments and professional and paraprofessional staff, and witnessed collection development practices at the branch and systemwide levels. By spending individual time with librarians in the children's services, adult services, and circulation departments, Michelle learned about the roles librarians play as department heads and supervisors and how they interact with their staff. She was present for program planning and attended special events, like teen poetry night and story times for toddlers. She observed how the children's librarian interacts with large and small audiences and deals with unruly children. She heard about new trends in services and technology being explored by the library.

While completing her internship, Michelle was also enrolled in a collection management course and so was especially interested in obtaining practical experience working with a collection. Linda suggested that she weed and acquire new materials for the science and history sections in the children's room. Using a "dusty books" list identifying titles that had not circulated in the past two years, Michelle began the process of selecting books for weeding. She recalls agonizing over which items to weed but eventually presented and successfully defended her choices and weeding criteria to the children's librarians and Linda. She then identified gaps in the science and history sections. By browsing catalogs, professional journals, and online vendor sources, Michelle compiled a list of titles and ISBNs recommended for purchase. Throughout this project, she became familiar with the library's acquisitions procedures, the role of technical services, the organization of the collection, and circulation procedures.

Working the reference desk gave Michelle practical patron experience and insight into the reality of serving a community consisting of people with differing needs. By learning how to do reference interviews and readers' advisory, and then actually using those skills while on a live desk, Michelle was able to get a clearer picture of what being a public service librarian is all about. Practical experience with serving people on demand certainly tests the skills and methods learned in the reference class!

Constant communication was vital to the internship experience. Linda facilitated communication by clearing and reserving part of her work space for Michelle. Because they were working in the same space, their opportunities for communication conveniently presented themselves each work day. In addition, Linda made herself accessible during the times Michelle was working on a project or reviewing what had been learned previously. A written schedule helped Michelle focus her time at the library during those fifteen weeks. Linda structured the internship so that each experience and discussion built on the last, until Michelle had a greater understanding of the library's policies, organization, and operations.

BECOMING A PROFESSIONAL

Looking back, Michelle observed that she had taken the practicum to gain a better perspective of actual librarianship, especially as related to her coursework. However, she took more from the internship than just a better perspective. Linda had shown her exactly what constitutes professional behavior and how personal opinions and philosophies can shape a collection, a position, a department, and even an entire library.

Not all students choose the distance learning option solely because they are involved in a career. Many students choose to participate in distance education because of their connections to family, home, and community. These students will most likely end up looking for a job locally, and having interned in the area may help them get a foot in the door when looking for professional work. Because distance learning students don't participate in traditional on-campus activities, it is essential that they do hands-on professional-level work during their internship. Weeding the collection, working the reference desk, attending staff meetings, making recommendations for collection purchases, and assisting with story time are all pieces of the practical, hands-on side of librarianship. These components of the practicum were complemented by such commonsense lessons as how to conduct oneself in staff or committee meetings and how to value janitorial and maintenance staff.

As students go through the internship process, they should not only concentrate on their own personal development but also pay attention to how they are being mentored and trained. Before Michelle knew it, she, now as a librarian, was teaching/assisting staff members and addressing the very same questions and problems she had asked Linda. As a supervisor, Michelle had learned from Linda the importance of communication and attention to detail. Adherence to a desk schedule and coordinating activities, such as programs and outreach, make for a less stressful and more harmonious staff. The internship taught her how to balance her own learning with the almost immediate role of teaching. Moreover, the internship prepared Michelle for her position as both a children's librarian and as second-in-charge at a small area library. She was judged, not just by her manager, but by the other staff members as well. Having a trainer observe the trainee and work toward a level of comfort is vital to new job success. In a library system where librarians are supervisors, the internship was the first step in learning the skills to instruct and supervise staff. Those skills proved to be immediate and necessary.

During the internship, Michelle was prompted to consider career paths and preferences. The practicum put working into context just as her current job has put the practicum into context—neither experience is as fruitful without the other. The internship gave Michelle the confidence she needed to apply for a professional position as a librarian without having any paid library experience. In addition, she has been able to draw upon and model Linda's attention to detail, her decorum with staff, peers, and superiors, and her qualities as a mentor. Being included behind the scenes and interacting with staff at work and in meetings has proven critical. When Michelle began her first job, she had to guess less about protocol: The environment was similar enough. A good internship is one that affords an opportunity to "do" the librarian's job. More importantly, the internship should make one aspire to be the mentor of a future intern.

• 11 •

Exploring Public Librarians' Many Roles through a Library System Internship, or How to Learn Thirty Jobs in as Many Days

Christine Dettlaff

When I look back on my public library internship, I am amazed not only at how much we managed to cram into five weeks, but also how much of what I learned was subsequently used in my professional work.

SETTING THE SCENE

I was nearing the end of library school when I decided to do an internship in a public library. I had been working for a year as a part-time media assistant in a school library and was fairly certain I did not want to become a school library media specialist. I thought the public library might be a better fit for me, so I decided to try a public library internship during the summer term.

I contacted my advisor, Dr. Kathy Latrobe, at the University of Oklahoma School of Library and Information Studies (SLIS) and told her I wanted to intern at a public library. To receive credit for an internship, SLIS students must work under the supervision of a professional librarian for 135 hours. Upon completing the internship, the student receives a grade of "satisfactory," plus three hours of credit, if all requirements are met. Dr. Latrobe very graciously agreed to set up an internship for me with the Pioneer Library System headquartered in Norman, Oklahoma. The Pioneer Library System is a multi-county system with nine branches located throughout central Oklahoma. My new supervisor was small branch/system services coordinator Peggy Cook, who supervises nine branch managers and is coordinator of outreach services to rural communities. She is also involved in a variety of administrative projects.

The library school sets general objectives for all internships, including applying principles and theories of library and information studies in a practical

95

work environment, supplementing knowledge in the student's specialization through hands-on experience, and evaluating a particular job situation. In addition to these, Dr. Latrobe and I set specific objectives for my upcoming experience in a public library system. The more specific objectives were:

> to gain an overview of how the library system functions as a whole;
> to observe formal and informal communication flows within the system;
> to understand how the system interacts with a variety of publics;
> to discover how in-service and continuing education are managed and encouraged within the system; and
> to examine the differences between school and public libraries.

My supervisor, Peggy Cook, and I then met to discuss activities that would help me meet these particular objectives. She felt the best way to meet the first three would be to observe branch managers and help with the day-to-day operations at each of the small branches. She also planned for me to spend some time in materials selection, cataloging, technical processing, and interlibrary loan. In the Pioneer Library System, these functions are all centralized within the main library.

MY INTERNSHIP

On the first day of my internship, Peggy introduced me to everyone at the main library and then presented me with the library's hefty policies and procedures manual, which I read between activities that first week. We further discussed the composition of the library's various staff work groups, as well as Pioneer's philosophy of employee empowerment.

The next day I attended a new employee orientation where, in addition to receiving useful background information about the Pioneer Library System, I became familiar with the layout of the main library during a walking tour. One section that was just emerging then was the young adult area. After the tour I talked briefly with library manager Susan Gregory about the new space and was advised to look at a teen's bedroom for ideas on designing a young adult area. Susan also suggested using teens as liaison with teachers and peers. This conversation turned out to be especially helpful when I later became a young adult librarian.

During the first week, Peggy and I visited four different branches. Among the highlights were sitting in on a story time and helping out at the children's reference desk in the main library. I also checked in learning kits, helped children and their parents find books and use computer CD-ROM games, gave out information about programs, and got to know many of the very talented and friendly children's librarians of the Norman Public Library. I found the one-on-one interaction with children much more enjoyable than trying to deal with a class of twenty-five all at once, as I had been doing in the school library.

The last day of that very busy first week I accompanied Peggy to a meeting of the state library's public librarian certification board. A good portion of Oklahoma's librarians do not have professional degrees. Therefore, the Oklahoma Department of Libraries offers a program in which public librarians can become certified by taking classes to improve their skills and train in new technologies. Peggy, who served on the certification board, knew I was interested in children's work and so introduced me to Donna Norvell, the state library's consultant for children's services. Donna became a great contact for me later as a children's librarian, especially when undertaking my first summer reading program on my own.

During week two, I spent a morning with Caroline Dulworth, who showed me how she catalogs books using the Dynix automation software, OCLC, and Dewey for Windows. She also taught me about authority work, a concept I had not understood well in my Organization of Information class in library school. It suddenly all became clear, however, as I watched Caroline check the authority list for duplication. I also talked with Anne Harris, one of the materials selectors for the Pioneer Library System, because I was curious about how she decided which books to order for each branch. She told me that selectors spend some time out in the branches, weeding the collections and working in public services to keep in touch with library patrons. They also chat with the branch librarians to find out what is being requested and what was needed that was not in the collection. Selectors each specialize in certain material formats, age levels, or genres. I also spent time in the interlibrary loan department and learned how the Pioneer Library System handles censorship challenges to materials. In addition, I got a taste of what it's like to be a library page. A progress meeting with Dr. Latrobe and Peggy revealed that the internship was going extremely well and that I was learning a lot.

During week three, I attended a senior management team meeting at the main library in Norman. Everyone made me feel welcome. I worked in four more branch libraries—each one a bit different, but all filled with wonderfully friendly staff members. I was invited to a staff luncheon at one of the branches and taken out for lunch by the manager at another branch. The Newcastle library manager, Kathie Thomas, taught me more about customer service than anyone has before or since. I use her suggestions even now when training my staff.

At the Tecumseh branch, I helped with a Stick-Horse Rodeo program (part of Oklahoma's award-winning *Yipee Yi Yo! Read Stampede!* summer reading program theme). Again, it was great fun for me coming in at the last minute as an extra helper. Only later did I realize how much work goes into planning and putting on such programs.

In the fourth week of my internship, I attended a Pioneer Library System board meeting. I worked in two more branch libraries, one of which was a joint school/public library in Purcell. I talked with manager Lisa Wells about combining the two types of libraries. She admitted that while it was challenging at times, on the whole she thought it worked fairly well despite occasional complaints about noise levels during class visits and concerns about children's access to adult-oriented materials.

It was during this week that Peggy mentioned a children's librarian vacancy at the El Reno Carnegie Library. I visited the library, sent the head librarian my résumé, was interviewed, and was hired as their new children's librarian! I had only one week off between the end of my internship and the beginning my first professional job.

WHAT I LEARNED

Were the objectives of the internship met? I would have to say that, yes, for the most part, they were. Working in all the different branches and spending time in centralized services gave me a great overview of how the system functions as a whole and how it serves a variety of patrons. Sitting in on meetings and talking with other librarians allowed me to experience formal and informal communication firsthand. It was obvious from the way so many people were willing to teach me what they did that the system values and encourages training. Finally, I observed two main differences between public and school libraries: (1) there is more of an emphasis on customer service in public libraries; and (2) children's services in public libraries are more entertainment-oriented than educational.

Peggy did an excellent job of providing me with a variety of experiences and introducing me to people who could give me different perspectives on their areas of library work. In fact, I believe the most significant thing I took away from the internship was the beginning of a network of colleagues. The people I met during my internship became my first all-important contacts in my professional work. I still run into some of these folks at conferences and meetings. And, of course, I'll always be indebted to Peggy for the tip that led to my first professional position.

Still, in hindsight, I realize I had become so caught up in all the great things the librarians did in the Pioneer system that I had neglected to ask people what they liked or disliked about their jobs. I didn't ask about salary, hours, or status—things that later became so important to me in terms of job satisfaction. Also, as I noted on my course evaluation, the number of on-the-job hours (135) required for the internship was excessive, especially for a five-week stretch. The last week of the internship was a whirlwind.

Overall, however, the internship was an invaluable experience and part of my library education that I wouldn't have wanted to miss. I am glad I did the internship late in library school, after I had taken classes in cataloging, materials selection, and library administration. These gave me the background needed to talk to people working in these areas and enabled me to observe how their job duties related to the theories and principles of library science. After all, it's easy to spout theories on exams and in papers, but much harder to see how they influence, even define, our daily tasks. An internship in a public library, or whatever kind of library one may choose, helps bring theory and practice into alliance.

• 12 •

Mentoring Library Technicians

Janet Larson and Jill Stockinger

$\mathcal{A}$lthough most librarians think of internships as something that graduate students undertake, some library technology programs also provide hands-on experience for course credit. A case in point is the Sacramento (California) City College (SCC) library information technology program, which places student interns in all types of libraries. In this chapter, we will describe SCC's highly effective internship program from the perspective of an educator as well as from that of a practicing librarian.

JANET'S STORY

As the former associate library director of the Sacramento Public Library, I was involved with the library information technology program at Sacramento City College for over twenty years as a guest speaker, mentor, and advisory board member. When I retired, I became a paid instructor in charge of the internship course, Library Technology 498: Work Experience in Library Information Technology.

Before graduating from our program, each student is required to work in a minimum of two libraries, either as an employee or as an intern. Library employees may earn 2.5 units of credit for 188 hours of work, while interns must work at two libraries for ninety hours each or 180 hours total of unpaid or volunteer work. Students may repeat the internship course once to learn new skills or increase work skills as a volunteer or beginning worker. In addition to the actual library work, each student is also required to keep a job journal, write a career essay, and prepare two periodical readings (one subject-oriented and the other career-related) as part of the course. Each must also pass a course midterm and final exam.

Although the student is responsible for setting up the internship, as course instructor I assist in finding suitable work sites, visit interns at their sites, and confer with the on-site supervisor. As required by the college, the instructor, the student, and the site supervisor enter into a formal agreement through a letter of cooperation and learning objective form. Each student must have at least three learning goals per site. Work hours and assignments, which should be varied and rotational rather than routine, are arranged between the student and the supervising librarian.

The broad goals of the LT-498 course are:

to build professional networks;
to provide hands-on experiences;
to build skill development and demonstrate these skills on the job;
to build self-confidence as a library employee; and
to confirm an interest in the library field.

Most of our students work outside the program, but not always in libraries. They represent a vast range of experience and ability; for several, English is a second language. For this reason, our students are now required to pass an English proficiency test before being placed at an internship site.

At times the students are overwhelmed with personal issues and need encouragement, reminders, and gentle prodding. Some require special dispensation—for example, starting an internship before the semester begins; taking an incomplete when unable to meet the course schedule; taking the midterm by mail when a child is ill; and accommodating library site problems, such as equipment failure, conflicting schedules, having a supervisor leave town because of an emergency, etc. We also spend time discussing job search strategies and how to compose cover letters and résumés. In addition, we do mock job interviews.

If they already work in a library, we encourage students to seek internship experiences in another type of library. Experienced students generally are assigned more difficult projects or tasks and are more able to work without direct supervision. Inexperienced students tend to start with simple tasks, such as shelving, periodical retrieval, and other clerical assignments. By the end of the internship, novices know how to check books in and out and register patrons. The smaller the library, the greater the variety of tasks they learn.

Recently, we placed interns in museums, schools, community colleges, universities, the state library, special libraries, and a variety of public libraries. One student interned at the public library near the school library where she works as a library technician. As a result, both agencies have joined forces to recruit newborns to get library cards, provide parents of preschool children with reading readiness information, and distribute adult literacy material. She also developed a self-help guide to the district-wide school catalog. Another student, who worked at a branch library, evaluated the use of books rotated to schools, discarded worn materials, and established an optimum number of books for rotation. She also identified and labeled teen science fiction materials and developed e-mail lists for notifying subscribers of upcoming library activities. To do this, she learned computer programs she had not used before.

Some librarians may be reluctant to take on students, saying that the time to train and supervise them does not make the experience worthwhile. However, so far all mentor supervisors have said that the students contribute to the library during their internship. In fact, most mentors are disappointed to learn that the class lasts only one semester. Jill's story below is typical of many of our internship experiences.

JILL'S STORY

The Sacramento Public Library (SPL), with its central facility and twenty-five branches, has benefited over the years from the work of interns. These have included both paid and unpaid positions. Paid internships are made available to SPL employees who are expected to continue with the library after they get their master's degree. Because, until recently, there was no library school nearby, very few staff members have taken advantage of this program. Far more common are the unpaid internships for non–SPL employees. In lieu of monetary compensation, these interns receive course credit toward their degrees. During the last four years, I helped supervise two interns at the Carmichael Regional Branch, located in the unincorporated area of Sacramento County. One student completed her internship while taking distance education classes through the San Jose State University School of Library and Information Science. The other, Anatoliy, was a young Russian-American student attending Sacramento City College.

Anatoliy had worked in a library in the Soviet Union for many years before coming to the United States. Here, he decided to obtain a degree from an American college to help him get a job similar to the one he had in the USSR. Among the several courses he took was Library Technology 498: Work Experience in Library Information Technology. This course was created to give students structured on-the-job training in Sacramento area libraries under the supervision of professional librarians. Before taking this class, he had to complete three core courses in library and information technology, in addition to being enrolled in at least seven units during the internship semester.

After formally agreeing to have Anatoliy work with us as a library assistant, we filled out the appropriate forms and proceeded to develop four objectives to be completed as part of his internship experience:

1. Master using the online public access catalog (OPAC) and perform three kinds of basic searches (author, title, and keyword), and master using several of the library's online sources, including the EBSCO magazine database.
2. Create a marketing plan to draw more Russian speakers into the library and advertise accordingly.
3. Develop a course outline and teach a class—in English and in Russian—on using the OPAC and library databases.
4. Use the library software (III/Millennium) to add books to the library database, to withdraw books, to upgrade records, and check in returned library material.

Anatoliy completed all these objectives successfully, including teaching a class to twelve Russian-speaking patrons which, in turn, helped us reach an important segment of our community. His time with us also helped him master the basic processes performed by library assistants. There was definitely mutual benefit in completing this internship. Library staff have encouraged Anatoliy to pursue a master's degree in library science.

III

NONTRADITIONAL PUBLIC LIBRARY INTERNSHIP SETTINGS

• 13 •

The Tribal Library Intern Project:
A Practicum in Cultural Lessons

Bonnie Biggs

 𝒯rom the mid-1970s to the mid-1980s a series of federal grants set the groundwork for the establishment of tribal libraries across the nation. During the 1960s, while libraries in the dominant culture were establishing "outreach" departments and finding ways to build bridges to heretofore neglected populations, librarian-educators Charles Townley and Lotsee Patterson lobbied and applied for federal monies to establish libraries on tribal lands. Townley and Patterson were among the first to take meaningful action toward the development of tribal libraries as Native American communities began to emerge from a totally oral tradition into one that sought to find ways to preserve, transfer, and disseminate cultural traditions through print and new media formats.

In 1984, Patterson helped write the legislation that amended the Library Services and Construction Act (LSCA) to include Title IV: Library Services for Indian Tribes and Hawaiian Natives Program. This legislation made possible the establishment of the first tribal libraries in San Diego County—a region that has more American Indian reservations than any other county in the United States. The San Diego County Library was awarded an LSCA grant to fund the Indian Library Services Project (ILSP), which helped establish tribal libraries, in 1987.

TRIBAL LIBRARIES: CURRENT CALIFORNIA HISTORY

To update the California State Library on the number, location, and status of tribal libraries in the state, I undertook a census and needs assessment of tribal libraries in 2000. This ten-month project involved visiting thirty-four reservations in five southern California counties (Imperial, Inyo, Riverside, San Bernardino, and San Diego). My objective was to find out which reservations had libraries, assess their status and needs, and report the findings to the California State Library. I discovered that:

> eighteen of the reservations visited had library facilities;
> fourteen of these library facilities had established open hours;
> seventeen of the libraries had an organized and accessible collection;
> only seven of the libraries had on-site, paid staff for library services;
> none of the paid library staff had a master's degree in library or information science or a California library media teacher credential; and
> only five of the reservations had an established funding base for library services. Of these libraries, only three received the majority of their funding from the tribe. Others were, like most tribal libraries, dependent on grants.

I also found that tribal librarians felt isolated and disconnected from other libraries in general and tribal libraries in particular. In addition, the need for basic library skills was frequently expressed by tribal library staff who had little or no training but were assigned the responsibility of running the reservation's library.

BUILDING BRIDGES

From its inception fourteen years ago, the California State University San Marcos has maintained positive relationships with local American Indian reservations. Linkages began through outreach activities that were centered in the library and initiated by David Whitehorse, a professor of American Indian Studies, and me. As the federal ILSP funds dried up, Dr. Whitehorse and I began a series of initiatives to pick up where the San Diego County Library project left off. We recognized that establishing relationships between the Indian community and the university had to be a careful, sensitive process. American Indian storytellings, American Indian cultural fairs, and American Indian pow-wows (there were several over the years) were precursor events that paved the way for developing meaningful ties with nearby tribal libraries. A small number of ILSP libraries remained vital, functioning institutions, while others struggled to survive as they competed with critical community services such as water and fire and police protection.

The Tribal Library Intern Project was specifically created to assist the valiant efforts of tribal library staff at the Rincon and Pala reservation libraries, situated in northern San Diego County some forty-five miles from the university. The project enables library school students to work, under my general supervision, in the tribal libraries, completing assignments that tribal library staff have identified as important.

Since years of work in gaining the Native community's trust could be ruined by one insensitive intern, cultural sensitivity training is a must. The interns learn that the mission, operation, and internal perception of a tribal library is markedly different from libraries in the macro-culture. In addition, they learn that tribal libraries tend to serve as the educational hub of the reservation, offering everything from Head Start story times to GED preparation and college extension courses. Tribal libraries also often serve as social gathering places or, in some cases, as museums. Those that serve the general or tribal population at large take a more holistic view of libraries in terms of place and service. The Indian value that places the good of the many before individual need is alive and operational in most tribal libraries.

To initiate the internship project, I contacted the associate director of the San Jose State University (SJSU) School of Library and Information Science's distance education program to inquire about the feasibility of placing interns in tribal libraries. Although the school's practicum course suited the objectives of the tribal libraries project, the associate director wanted to ensure that the students would not be used just as "free labor." Instead, she wanted to place them in situations that would offer a substantive learning experience. As a university librarian, I was most interested in having the interns share their emerging knowledge with the fledgling libraries. The associate director agreed and posted an announcement in the student newsletter.

ON-THE-JOB CHALLENGES

The Rincon reservation is located in north central San Diego County on eight square miles of green valley and foothills. The on-reservation population numbers 1,600 people, with 651 of those enrolled as members of the San Luiseño band of Mission Indians. The tribal library was established within the Rincon tribal hall through the Indian Library Services Project in 1987. Since that time the library has seen six library managers come and go and has changed tribal councils a dozen times and tribal administrators five times. The never-ending battle between the U. S. government and Indian tribes over sovereignty and economic independence renders the reservation's political climate unpredictable at best. At the onset of the Tribal Library Intern Project, the Rincon library and its staff were stable. That would soon change, however, as the project—not to mention the interns—were tested and strengthened in the process.

Before the first internship, the student and I visited the tribal library, where I introduced her to tribal hall staff and then left her to work out the details of her assignments with the library manager. The intern was to work with the tribe to identify an appropriate software system for their small collection and services. However, the tribe ended up having larger issues to contend with that summer. Shortly before the internship began, the Rincon reservation opened its casino, featuring four hundred video gaming machines which, at the time, were considered illegal. On the intern's first day of work, the tribal library manager informed her that he had to leave to videotape the opening of the casino and the expected arrest of tribal elders. Needless to say, the intern was unable to work with the library manager that day and quickly began to understand how the complexity of tribal politics takes precedence over daily operations of any agency on the reservation. A federal order prohibiting the use of the video machines was imposed, and the casino's business began a fast decline. Later that summer all tribal staff hours were reduced and employees were laid off. The tribal library manager was unable to interact consistently with the intern and eventually left the reservation. The practicum was uneven at best, resulting in the intern losing the opportunity to do the work and the considerable tuition paid for the course!

PROJECT EXPANSION

The Pala reservation, only five miles from Rincon, is inhabited mostly by descendants of the Cupeño people, who were relocated by the federal government in 1902 from nearby Warner Hot Springs. The Pala library was established by tribal initiative in 1989. The library manager, a Luiseño woman who was enrolled in a local library technology certificate program, was well regarded by the tribal council members even though she came from another reservation and was not Cupeño. The site was perfect for an internship because of its stability and the library manager's desire for an intern to help in the areas of automation, cataloging, and planning a new library.

I met with two potential interns to go over tribal histories, politics, and culture and to give them an overview of the university's relationship, to date, with local reservations and their libraries. The students exhibited curiosity and genuine interest in the project. As interns they proved to be perfect cultural ambassadors for both their library school and the California State University San Marcos. They assisted the tribe in drafting a proposal to the Department of Education for the Library Services for Indian Tribes and Hawaiian Natives Program Special Projects Grants. They also participated in a Cupa Cultural Days event, ate their first fry bread, and adopted two starving and wounded "rez dogs," all while embracing these experiences with enthusiasm and grace. Daily journals kept by the interns document the life-changing experience they had on the reservation. Sarah Way, one of the first interns, noted in her journal:

> I think that it is very interesting to be the minority for a bit. I think it would help increase everyone's sensitivity. However, I still know that when I leave the reservation I am immediately back in the world where I am the majority. Everyone has been very nice to me, but then I expected them to be. I was thinking today that most minorities cannot make that assumption. That's a very sad thing.

The first two interns set the standard for the project. They joined the SJSU associate director and me on a panel discussion at the California Library Association annual conference. Although neither student had ever presented at a professional conference before, they both came alive and delivered a stirring account when telling their stories. The thirteen interns who have followed also found their own unique ways to embrace cultural lessons and opportunities. Intern Girija Karamcheti, who lost her home in a recent wildfire, notes in her journal:

> We keep wanting to go home. It is the place, that little plot of land, that keeps calling to us and it feels as though we are lost, as though we have lost who we are, because it is tied to that physical location. I feel as though this is what may be felt by Native Americans who were moved from their homelands.

MISSION ACCOMPLISHED

The Tribal Library Intern Project remains alive and well. The tremendous success of the program can be measured by the learning outcomes of the interns and the value added to the tribal library. Since the project began, fifteen different interns have served internships in the Pala library. As working professionals, several have even returned to complete special projects—gratis—for Pala. Since the program's onset, interns have assisted in setting up an automated system for cataloging, acquisitions, and circulation; cataloged gift materials; designed components of the new building; moved the library; developed a patron usage and assessment of services survey; helped to write a collection development policy and plan; weeded the collection; worked with the university's cataloging librarian to revise and improve cataloging practices; worked with the university's systems librarian to research automated system software for a proposed upgrade; designed a website; and helped define technology needs for a cultural preservation project. When asked how the Tribal Library Intern Project has impacted the Pala tribal library, library manager Doretta Musick says, "It has meant everything. They have helped us to become a real library over the years—I can't say enough about how important this project has been for our development."

HOW TO DEVELOP A TRIBAL LIBRARY INTERNSHIP

Developing internships in tribal libraries can provide life-changing experiences for students entering the profession. The intern benefits by experiencing a degree of cultural immersion and by contributing to the operational goals of the tribal library. Most importantly, the student gains a broader perspective of libraries and how they differ—in particular, how tribal libraries serve as social gathering places, as the educational hub of the reservation, and as centers for the oral transmission of knowledge and cultural traditions.

If you are interested in developing a similar project in your library's service area, there are a few things to consider. Is there a master's of library and information science degree–granting institution in your service area? If there is, find out if the curriculum includes internship opportunities and, if so, how the site's supervisory role is defined. Besides the tribal library manager, someone will need to assume overall responsibility and be the liaison between the library school and the tribal library. Is there an Indian reservation or sizable Indian population in your library's service area? If so, you'll want to make contact with the governing body—likely a tribal council—to determine if there is a tribal library. If there is, you'll want to begin to connect with the tribal library staff and tribal council to determine their interest in an intern program. You should expect to spend most of your time, perhaps several visits, listening. Ask yourself why you and your institution would want to pursue this kind of program in the first place. Beyond altruism, does your institution hold a strong commitment to community outreach? Are there compelling, mission-based reasons for engaging in projects that center on multicultural issues? Are there people within the library whose job description or research naturally link them to this kind of activity? If so, will your administrators support the time commitment required to develop and then oversee an intern program?

When all is said and done, the value added on both sides of such a relationship has tremendous potential. Think of the words of Chief Joseph, in 1877, on the death of Looking Glass and the imprisonment of the Nez Perce: "Let us now put our heads together and see what kind of life we can make for our children."

ACKNOWLEDGMENTS

I would like to acknowledge Dr. Nancy Burns and Dr. Debra Hansen of the San Jose State University School of Library & Information Science; Dr. Cindy Mediavilla; pioneer interns Kim Laru and Sarah Way, and all other interns from SJSU; tribal library staff Doretta Musick, Mark Macarro, and Patrick Viveros for their commitment to this project; and Dr. David Whitehorse for the initial inspiration to follow this path.

Literacy Internships:
Take a Plunge into the Deep End

Taylor Willingham

I feel obliged to "come clean" about my own biases regarding library school internships in literacy programs. My perspective is based on the decade I spent as the director of a large and dynamic library-based literacy program and as founding member of the American Library Association's Committee on Literacy. As current adjunct lecturer for the library schools at both the University of Illinois and the San Jose State University (SJSU), I have a profound passion for library-based literacy and definite ideas about what constitutes a successful internship.

I believe that a library internship should provide students with: (1) a testing ground for the theoretical frameworks they study in academia; (2) an environment where they may apply the skills they develop during their educational pursuits; (3) the opportunity to develop new skills under practical, real-life conditions; and (4) an environment where they may test new and old theories about the role of libraries in society. As I will discuss below, library literacy programs are ideally suited to meet these criteria. And yet, if the meager response to my calls for real-life internship examples is any indication, these opportunities have been grossly underutilized by library academia. In this chapter, I will document the rich internship opportunities that literacy programs can offer.

WANTED: LIBRARY DIRECTOR. INTERNS ONLY, PLEASE.

Imagine that you have just been charged with establishing a library in a room that is starkly furnished with plastic chairs, heavy wooden tables, and a few bookshelves cluttered with cheap, tattered, paperback romance novels. You will complete this assignment without a budget or staff, and your every action will be closely monitored. The library will be serving low-literate and skeptical patrons who would prefer to spend afternoons playing volleyball and horseshoes rather than face possible ridicule from their peers if they *do* grace your door. You will also be held to strict accountability and outcome measures; your license to operate the library will continue only as long as you demonstrate that your target population is learning to read.

This is the situation that SJSU student Elaine Wong faced as an intern for Santa Clara County (California) Library's Reading Program. Operating under contract to the State Department of Correction to provide inmate literacy services, the Reading Program promised to raise a prison library/literacy center like a phoenix from neglected ashes. It was up to Elaine to bring the vision of inmate literacy project supervisor Julie Jacobs into reality.

Undaunted, Elaine recruited inmate trustees, who could read, to be library assistants or peer tutors. She conducted outreach campaigns to entice skeptical potential library users to spend their "yard time" in the library learning to read. She rescued materials discarded by local public libraries and rallied the community to contribute quality literature to this haphazard collection. Along with her newly trained library assistants, she developed a circulation system that would mystify most librarians but served the needs of the inmates.

Let us carefully consider the skills that this situation demanded. The inmate literacy learners were not only struggling to overcome limited literacy skills, they were doing so under less than conducive and potentially hostile conditions. First, let us consider the percentage of the general population that faces stigma or other barriers to the vast resources of the library. It is probably a larger number than you can fathom. We know, for example, that 40 percent of the population at large read below the eighth-grade level. Does this population readily look to the library—the place that houses thousands of inaccessible books—as a place of learning and refuge? Then, consider that the literacy rates of inmates are *significantly* lower than the general population (60 to 80 percent read below the eighth-grade level). This, while simultaneously housed in an environment where admitting *any* kind of weakness takes tremendous courage. Suddenly you begin to appreciate the immensity of the outreach task that Elaine faced.

Next consider the political astuteness and interpersonal skills this position required. Public librarians who were reticent about contributing discarded items had to be assured that new procedures would be worth the extra effort because they would extend the useful life of these materials. Skeptical correctional officers had to be convinced that the library was a nonthreatening and worthwhile endeavor, and that it would not compromise their ability to maintain order. Community volunteers and contributors had to be courted and convinced to donate time and resources. And inmates, who had been subject to ridicule when faced with the printed word, had to feel safe and confident but not coerced. This internship required an ability to convince complex bureaucracies to work together to achieve a noble end.

Consistent with a learner-centered approach, Elaine was determined that the library would reflect the needs of the inmates. She therefore had to be flexible and, in some cases, to abandon what she had learned in school about collection development and cataloging. The trustees were entrusted to organize the collection in a manner that suited the users' needs. Lacking a budget for materials or staff, Elaine had to develop creative strategies to meet the needs of this special population. Her challenges included limited resources, lack of visible support, inadequate space, no staff, an uneducated volunteer force, no materials, a burdensome bureaucracy, and a very short time period in which to demonstrate success according to strict accountability standards.

Miraculously, the phoenix rose from these haphazard ashes. While the end product would hardly conjure up the images that most librarians, correctional officers, members of the public, or even the inmates themselves would equate with a library, it fulfilled its core mission to bring quality literature to users in an easily accessible format, while attending to the needs of those whose literacy skills, even under the best of circumstances, would have prevented access to this material. Pick your metaphor, but this was a baptism by fire, an intense on-the-job experience, a plunge into the deep end of the swimming pool. Fortunately, Elaine was not alone in her efforts. She had the unwavering support and superior guidance of her visionary supervisor, Julie Jacobs.

Hard-core, tattoo-laden gang members, drug addicts, petty thieves, and multi-term armed robbers read and discussed quality literature, met distinguished authors, and wrote poetry and essays that were subsequently published in "Emerging Voices," Santa Clara County Library's annual collection of literacy student contributions. Inmates who could read well participated in a peer tutor training program and spent sunny afternoons in the library tutoring and encouraging fellow inmates, who struggled to decipher the squiggles in their workbooks.

OTHER EXAMPLES FROM THE FIELD

The opportunity to actually establish and direct a library like the one described above is unusual; but there is no shortage of exciting internships offered by literacy programs. Since literacy programs often seek external funding for special projects and cultivate a close and intimate relationship with the tutors and learners in their program, an internship could include grant writing and management, project management, adult literacy student intake interviews, family literacy programming, tutor training, volunteer management, event planning, collection development, outcomes-based evaluation, report-writing, public relations and outreach, newsletter development, and public speaking. Literacy programs thrive on collaboration with community agencies, giving student interns the opportunity to also learn about their community and how to create collaborative projects that are mutually beneficial.

When University of California, Los Angeles (UCLA), library student Christine McQuown interned with the Santa Fe Springs Public Library's literacy program, her duties were broadly defined. She helped the administrators with planning, documentation, publicity, children's story times, and school visits, *and* she was a tutor. Christine, who had extensive experience producing television shows, reflected on her role in managing the family literacy services. "This is not something that a new librarian in management should be asked to take on," she explained. "It takes a lot to administer that kind of program in terms of management skills and literacy knowledge." These were the skills that she gained and applied in a supportive environment under the supervision of literacy director Jerry Edwards, her capable and respected mentor.

Although not a library intern, Lynnette Hawkins, an AmeriCorps volunteer, had an opportunity that could easily be described as a library student's dream internship. As the manager of the Writers to Readers project, Lynnette organized brunches at the library where learners met with distinguished authors. Lynnette coordinated their speaking engagements with the SJSU Center for Literary Arts. She also developed writing workshops and compiled information to prepare the learners for their meeting with the authors. She developed a writing contest for learners, organized volunteer judges, and arranged for the publication of a collection of learner essays. What library school student wouldn't be thrilled to meet distinguished authors, such as poets Carolyn Forche, Yusef Komunyakaa and Ginny Lim, grand dames of the literary world Tillie Olson and Grace Paley, Mexican American poet Juan Felipe Herrera, and Native American poet/musician Joy Harjo? When the learners saw author Mary Gordon tear up while reading a manuscript about her father, all reticence and self-consciousness evaporated. Learners spontaneously reached for their workbooks and began sharing their own stories about their families. Would this not be a magical moment that would last an intern a lifetime?

Other literacy programs report that interns have developed résumé-writing courses, managed computer sites, conducted family literacy programs, managed the literacy collection, conducted reading assessments, led in-service workshops, and monitored donations.

Why should library schools pay attention to internship opportunities in literacy programs? At a time of dwindling resources, librarians need to become fund-raisers, capacity-builders, and "social entrepreneurs." Library directors must use new and creative ways to rally community support. Libraries will need to reach out to *all* members of the community, including nontraditional library users whose resources are limited because of life circumstances or language and literacy abilities. These are strategies and practices that literacy programs, by necessity, have been engaged in for the past few decades. Furthermore, literacy programs offer students the opportunity to develop skills and work in an environment that will position them to respond to emerging trends in the library field and prepare them for the duties they will fulfill as librarians. Literacy programs provide a model for the growing number of libraries that are taking their place as community builders and affirming their civic, educational, and democratic mission.

LIBRARY STUDENT PERSPECTIVES

Perhaps the strongest case for literacy program internships comes from the library students themselves. After five years of teaching seminars for San Jose State University, I am struck by the enthusiasm of the students and their passion for literacy. When Blanche Woolls, the director of the School of Library and Information Science, first asked me to teach the class, she warned me that it might be canceled for lack of interest. Not only was there interest, the students came from great distances to participate in the four-weekend course, even incurring travel and hotel costs. They represented high school libraries, a vocational college, and children's services. Their interests included homelessness, alcohol/drug recovery, racism, and jail library services. They all saw literacy as integral to the work they were doing and to their future roles. Many even argued that literacy should be a required library school course.

Of the nineteen students who participated in that first class, four decided to pursue literacy as a career choice and two volunteered to help incarcerated adult learners at the county correctional facility's library. One student was hired by the Santa Clara County Library's literacy program and conducted focus groups with adult learners to determine what makes a learner-friendly library. Another student decided to incorporate literacy into his focus on library services for the homeless. One student was hired by the Oakland Public Library's Second Start program. Still another, interested in services for senior citizens, made literacy the topic of research papers for other classes and was still posting information about literacy and seniors on the school's electronic discussion board long after he graduated.

The literacy seminar at SJSU has never been canceled for lack of interest. In fact, one course (before I realized I could set registration limits) had fifty-six students! These future librarians will be advocates for literacy within their own communities and library systems and will be a voice for the learners who need their services—not bad outcomes for a class no one thought would garner support!

CULTIVATING TOMORROW'S LEADERS

When asked why she chose the Santa Fe Springs literacy program for her internship, UCLA student Christine McQuown replied, "I just believe in libraries and community hubs—community partners and libraries as a responsive service. Don't look at libraries in terms of books, but in terms of people. The library can help people attain goals." She then added that "reading is one of the ways that people can get to where they want to go—whatever that means to them!"

For Christine, the real benefit of the literacy internship was the opportunity to interact personally with the learners and their children, an experience that unfortunately none of her classmates had in their internships. As Christine notes, "The best way to be a great librarian is to know your patrons. When the family literacy program goes on for years and years, and the kids grow up, you are part of the community. You are interacting with those kids. The days of libraries as insular institutions are over; it's about really knowing and responding to your community."

The leaders of literacy programs, by virtue of their need to seek alternative funding sources and to support a population with multiple information needs that may fall outside of the library's expertise, are experts at knowing about the variety of community services and organizations. Such programs have partnered with community technology centers, Head Start, local theater groups, service agencies like the Lions and Rotary clubs, Toastmasters, leadership groups, corporate community liaisons, human resource departments, county correctional facilities, substance abuse programs, community policing agencies, the county registrar of voters, civic leagues, the League of Women Voters, history museums, youth service agencies, homeless shelters, battered women's shelters, work release programs, neighborhood associations, and federal housing agencies.

In 2003, READ/San Diego, the adult literacy program of both the San Diego Public Library and the San Diego County Library, was chosen by the U.S. Department of Education's Office of Vocational and Adult Education as one of twelve promising community partnerships that support adult education.

Under the inspirational leadership of Chris McFadden, READ/San Diego has established over two hundred community partnerships with churches, private companies, community-based organizations, government agencies, and drug and alcohol rehabilitation centers. Over sixty groups donate space for tutoring learners through the program. In addition, READ/San Diego runs highly successful workplace literacy programs at the City of San Diego's water and metro wastewater departments, Sea World, and Solar Turbines. Neighborhood learning centers provide extended hours and flexible scheduling for adults when they can't access one of the city or county's sixty-nine libraries.

RECOMMENDATIONS FOR THE FUTURE

So how do we create these rich learning opportunities for library students? Reflecting on her ten-week internship in Santa Fe Springs, Christine noted that the most gratifying aspect of her internship was hands-on experience with the patron/learners and their children. She was clear that she wanted the opportunity to make a difference, to see people evolve. She compared her literacy experience with other types of library internships and recognized that, as a librarian, she might not ever see the results of what she does. "People come in and you help them, but you may never know what happened," Christine observed. "In the literacy program, you develop relationships and you see the change over the long term. You are helping people reach their goals."

Valerie Hardie, of READ/San Diego, echoes Christine's sentiments. "Make it meaningful for volunteers by having them interact with the clients," she urges. "There is a balance between menial or clerical tasks, but there is always work with the clients. Interns should not be shoved in a corner just to file."

Other literacy program directors stressed the importance of negotiating clear objectives that mutually serve the interests of the student while meeting the needs of the organization. Hardie advises, "The person supervising must have a good sense of what needs to be done and be good at delegating and defining what can be taken away from staff. Organizing takes time."

Library literacy programs may not be taking full advantage of the talent and skills that library student interns have to offer. By the same token, it is likely that literacy has not been given fair consideration by students and their academic advisors. While the experience may not appeal to all students, literacy programs clearly provide exciting opportunities for students to apply the theory they learn in school and to develop close relationships with "unlikely" library patrons. A literacy internship may well provide the best training ground for future librarians.

Internships in Public Library Archives and Local History Collections

Lori A. Lindberg and Natalie K. Munn

*I*nternships—or practica, as they are sometimes called—in libraries with local history or archival collections can both strengthen local history and archives efforts and provide interns with valuable mentor relationships. Through interviews with librarians, archivists, and internship/practicum students and coordinators, this chapter documents success stories and offers advice to public librarians who would like to create meaningful internship opportunities in archives and local history. All the subjects we interviewed agree that internships offer valuable professional experience to library students interested in these special areas. Moreover, archives and local history career paths require expertise developed over time, via mentor relationships or apprenticeships, to supplement what is learned in a seminar or classroom environment.

BACKGROUND

San Francisco city archivist Susan Goldstein, an intern supervisor for eight years at the San Francisco Local History Center, part of the San Francisco Public Library, notes the differences in internship duties and learning experiences for those interns interested in local history or archives. "Unlike other public library internships, one in local history and archives means that the intern will be working with non-book materials, including archives and manuscript collections, ephemera, maps, and photographs, among other formats," she says. "All of these materials have special conservation, organization, and description needs, separate from standards used in the library world for books and periodicals. An internship in local history may also mean preparing an exhibit or other activities that are more museum-related."

Because there is no single credential path for an archivist or local history librarian, it is optimistic to assume that students graduating from library schools have all of the skills and experience necessary to become practicing professionals. Mindful of this reality, most professional archives positions require an undergraduate and a graduate degree, along with archival course work and a practicum. The Society of American Archivists (SAA) specifically addresses practical experience in its *Guidelines for a Graduate Program in Archival Studies* (available at http://www.archivists.org/prof-education/ed_guidelines.asp), stating that a practicum "allows students to verify their understanding of archival principles by applying them in real-life situations and to understand how to make adjustments so that archival principles fit archival practice." Furthermore, the SAA specifies that practica should be designed "by faculty in collaboration with the designated host institution's internship supervisor and include provision for regular feedback and evaluation."

INTERNS VERSUS VOLUNTEERS

Lori Lindberg, faculty supervisor for archives practicum students at San Jose State University's School of Library and Information Science, points out that being an intern's mentor is different from the job of a volunteer coordinator. Mentors should be committed to their students and have a vested interest in the practicum learning experience. They should be present and mentoring during 30 to 40 percent of the practicum and be familiar with the course content of the school the student attends. For example, the Museum of Local History, an all-volunteer organization in Fremont, California, offers project-oriented summer internship opportunities. Degreed adult volunteers coordinate these internships, which are overseen by a trained volunteer.

It is important to distinguish between volunteer opportunities and for-credit internship work. As the Bancroft Library's Jane Rosario explains, "The main difference between a volunteer experience and an internship is that the internship is deliberately designed as a learning experience, not just a working experience. We view internships as an opportunity to tutor young professionals and encourage them to continue in the archival profession." To accomplish this, Rosario strives to provide her interns with an experience that is broad, varied, and as intellectually stimulating as possible—including training and tours of the Bancroft and other repositories. She also includes interns in departmental meetings, so they can have a better understanding of work in the "real world." "An internship is a two-way street," Rosario explains. "We get work from them, and they get experience and education from us."

THE ROLE OF A MENTOR

Achieving benefits that are truly reciprocal requires a commitment to the interns. Mentoring organizations need to make sure they offer sufficient training opportunities and staff time devoted to instruction, observation, and feedback. Institutions need to offer relevant projects or supervised on-the-job responsibilities similar to what the students will encounter in their professional careers. They must also provide a pleasant work environment to fulfill the interns' needs. Ideally, their work should interface with their academic curriculum so they can put classroom learning into practice.

Jane Rosario stresses the importance of preparation, noting that significant time must be spent planning for the internship by:

creating projects for the intern to work on;
developing a training regimen;
setting aside dedicated workspace for the intern;
assigning a supervisor for the intern;
arranging tours and other educational opportunities, including inviting the intern to attend departmental meetings, events and training; and
encouraging the intern's professional development by discussing career goals, membership in professional associations, and contributions such as writing articles, etc.

Internships give students an opportunity to connect one-to-one with professional archivists and local history librarians who are willing to become mentors and advocates. Nannette Bricker-Barrett, librarian and mentor at the San Bernardino County Library, explains that "a good mentor is one who wants you to succeed and helps you achieve your goals." Paul Signorelli of the San Francisco Public Library suggests "that good mentors must be well-versed in their field, enthusiastic, patient, willing to listen as much as to respond, be interested in education and in learning while mentoring, and be aware of the important role they play in inspiring others to pursue the same career that the mentor is enjoying." Jane Rosario adds that a mentor must have "good communication and organizational skills as well as an affinity for the larger profession."

The relationship interns develop with their mentors provides them with valuable references as they interview for their first jobs or embark on career changes. Practicum student Mary Christine Devinney discovered that a great mentor is someone who becomes a professional ally when one is job hunting. Practicum mentors make good references because they are familiar with a job seeker's positive qualities and can cite personal examples of how an applicant has applied strengths in the working environment.

Devinney also found that having a good mentor is essential to the internship experience. "The great mentors work with the student, not only at the beginning to explain what is expected, but along the way, offering advice and encouragement," she says. "Good mentors can, and do, see potential problems before they become a problem and help the student learn ways to avoid common mistakes." According to Paul Signorelli, "Mentors should bring a high degree of professionalism and energy to their work with students. They should set the sort of example they wish they had (or actually did have) when they were learning their profession or moving from one level to another on their own career paths."

MENTOR CREDENTIALS

We asked interviewees whether a good mentor should be credentialed. This is often a point of contention, given the unusual career paths taken by many archivists and local history librarians. "The archivists in our repository have master's degrees in library science as well as history," Rosario explains.

> But given the many ways that people have entered the archival profession—and some are very good, knowledgeable archivists, too—one may not want to define "mentor" so narrowly. In general, as we move toward greater professionalization, it would be beneficial for the mentor to have a master's in library and information science (MLIS), have a master's degree in history with archival training, or be a certified archivist.

Nannette Bricker-Barrett agrees that mentors of library school students should be degreed professionals. "In addition to the knowledge base the degree brings to the relationship," she says, "the degree indicates the dedication to the profession that a mentor should have." Paul Signorelli reiterates the point: "Mentors should, at a minimum, have the same (or equivalent) credentials/degrees their students will need to find employment in their chosen field."

Former intern and now practicing librarian Rebecca Guillan believes that a library mentor should be degreed and notes that a good mentor is "someone available to talk about the project and share professional knowledge and experiences—someone who has authority."

THE COMPENSATION DILEMMA

We asked mentors, practicum students, and interns about paid internships and found (not surprisingly) that compensation ranges from an hourly market-rate pay scale budgeted annually and supervised by degreed librarians, to uncompensated programs with no budget that are staffed with noncredentialed volunteer mentors. This being said, even though the majority of internship/practicum opportunities are unpaid, most institutions have no problem filling them. As Signorelli notes, "Some interns receive stipends that reimburse them for the tuition fees they pay the university to complete a practicum; this obviously helps defray a little of the cost of their education, but doesn't seem to have much impact on whether students apply for internships at the San Francisco Public Library."

There is no doubt, though, that adult students in graduate degree programs deserve special consideration. In fact, most students are unable to leave their regular jobs to take on unpaid internship work. "Paid practicum students are better equipped to offer the institution their full attention," former intern Mary Christine Devinney explains. "The institution gets a better quality job out of an intern who is not working an additional full-time job to pay the bills." Jane Rosario agrees. "In recent years, all of our interns have been paid, and it is quite beneficial," she says. "There is greater accountability and the interns do feel valued. We like our interns to be committed to us and we are fortunate at this point in time to be able to commit to them by paying them."

The Fremont Local History Museum sweetens their internships with a stipend. Participating students are typically college-bound high school students or undergraduate college students exploring potential careers in museums, libraries, or archives. Because the majority of the museum's summer interns also hold other jobs, the museum finds that offering a stipend attracts dedicated interns who are willing to commit to a schedule and make the internship a priority.

SETTING UP AN INTERNSHIP PROGRAM

A well-planned practicum experience offers benefits regardless of the size of the project or scale of the program. An institution may want to start small with only one or two interns a year and then expand the scope of the program. If so, consider including budgeted internships in project grant proposals and/or in the organization's annual budget. Budgeting for practicum programs offers an organization the opportunity to regularly evaluate the reciprocal benefits of an internship, while also examining whether these benefits would be enhanced by more funding and/or staffing.

San Francisco Public Library (SFPL) currently budgets intern stipends and offers an average of four practica a year—one or two students are in archives, one is in the children's department, and one is in access services. These opportunities are very popular, in part because they offer a tuition reimbursement stipend. Because the practicum application process is highly competitive, it is organized by SFPL's human resources division, assuring impartial, uniform, and fair treatment of all practicum applications. According to the library's personnel analyst Paul Signorelli, success is guaranteed by:

> providing job descriptions that outline the positions to be filled;
> recruiting appropriately—SFPL publicizes openings at the San Jose State University (SJSU), for example, since MLIS students are perfect for the library's internship program;
> being responsive and providing timely updates to prospective interns during the selection process;
> providing well-focused orientations, where participants learn about the workplace and have a chance to meet with key personnel before beginning an internship; and
> providing written guidelines. At SFPL interns receive a manual that describes workplace policies. They also receive a written confirmation of the duties they will be expected to complete during their time at SFPL.

Because students pay money (i.e., tuition) to participate in an internship, librarians should ask themselves whether they have made every reasonable effort to make the intern's commitment of time and money worthwhile. As Jane Rosario emphasizes, "We try to give our interns as broad an experience as possible. We try to design the project to be a 'soup-to-nuts' experience."

FITTING THE INTERN INTO THE WORKFLOW

Good internships bring a fresh perspective to the organization and offer a win-win approach to tackling archival and local history projects. Such projects may include:

> cataloging and "cleaning up" catalog records;
> digitizing content;
> creating or marking up finding aids;
> conservation;
> creating exhibits;
> processing collections;
> rehousing collections; and
> reference/research.

At San Francisco Public Library, interns process collections, prepare finding aids, and create MARC records. "It's not necessary to create 'make-work' for interns," archivist Susan Goldstein admonishes. "There are ongoing functions in an archive that can always use assistance. I had an intern create a prototype for our first website in Special Collections. This was an excellent project that used this intern's computer skills to create something we really needed. I've also had interns organize ephemera files and conduct research in order to complete their tasks."

In 1997, the San Bernardino County Library was ready to embark on a "history of the library" archives project, but did not have enough staff to carry it out. Nannette Bricker-Barrett packaged the project so that a library school student could perform the required tasks. "Identify a finite and concrete aspect of a local history project that can be completed in the internship time frame and can be done in fits and starts to accommodate the student's schedule," she advises. "Your project needs to have some curriculum-based appeal—not always simple! Many of the projects that we would have loved to have an intern help with were very practical, but didn't fit well with academic/theoretical course work. So, there were no takers." Bricker-Barrett ended up listing her practicum project with SJSU's southern campus library program and was matched with Becky Guillan, then a library school student. Guillan worked with papers, documents, and photos all dealing with the library's history; sorted them by branch or historical incident; arranged the material chronologically; placed the items in the proper archival receptacle; and indexed the material by topic so that it could be easily accessed. According to Bricker-Barrett,

> We didn't know how to preserve the materials and had no time to learn how, so our intern was teaching *us* about preservation. Other types of volunteers may bring time and enthusiasm to a project, but not necessarily the professional knowledge of an educated intern.

SOME FINAL ADVICE

When asked to offer some final words of wisdom for libraries and librarians who might consider offering internships in local history and archives, the respondents shared common advice. Most offered words of encouragement and enthusiasm for their programs and the resulting benefits. Becky Guillan urged librarians to not be afraid of offering an MLIS student the opportunity to work on a project, because that intern could very well become a future employee. Paul Signorelli encouraged mentors to "think about what you would want if you were an intern, and provide that to yours." The Bancroft Library's Jane Rosario eloquently added:

> Make sure you have the time and space for interns. Make sure you want them. Make sure that you have an interested and dedicated mentor for each intern. Do not simply expect to squeeze work out of interns: it is a two-way street. If you are a mentor, be prepared to give of yourself—your time, your energy, your knowledge, your experience, and your enthusiasm for the profession. Remember that these young professionals will be your future colleagues.

· *16* ·

One Special Collection, Many Personal Paths

Elaine Meyers, Christie Peterson, and Alicia Sugiyama

$\mathscr{T}$he Phoenix Public Library's Center for Children's Literature exemplifies the riches provided by a large urban public library. Located in the Burton Barr Central Library, the Center for Children's Literature (CCL) provides public display areas for rotating exhibits on the art of children's literature. It also contains a noncirculating collection of approximately three thousand books, plus numerous pieces of original art, manuscript items, posters, and ephemera organized into distinct collections related to children's literature. The center's largest assemblage by far is the historical collection, which seeks to preserve historically important works of children's literature following the guidance of Cornelia Meigs's *Critical History of Children's Literature* (Macmillan, 1969). The other collections within CCL include the Newbery and Caldecott winners, books on Arizona, books written by children-as-authors, pop-up books, folktales, and bibliographies. The vision for the Center is a rich archive for research and a dynamic public space to promote children's literature to aspiring writers, artists, and students of all ages.

The value of CCL is undisputed. But like art and music in public education, when times are tough special collections fall to the bottom of the list for staffing and funding. Historically, the Center has relied on graduate library school interns for staffing and on private funding for acquisitions. The Friends of the Phoenix Public Library and the library's foundation have provided funding for acquisitions and exhibit support, but the day-to-day maintenance of the collection has fallen in large part to graduate library school interns. One of the most attractive aspects of CCL internships is the ability of the students to personalize their learning objectives within the rich scope of collections and programs offered by the Center. Some of our previous interns, who currently hold leadership positions in area school and public libraries, still use the information gained during their internships. The opportunities presented to the graduate students are rich, and the benefits gained by the Phoenix Public Library are invaluable.

We would like to share the stories of two of our most recent interns in the Center for Children's Literature. One is the story of an internship used to refine career goals, and the second is the story of a student's final semester at the University of Arizona's School of Information Resources and Library Science. We will end this chapter with a look at the plans for our next two interns and see how the CCL work continues to meet the goals of graduate students and the library alike.

CHRISTIE'S EXPERIENCE

I'm a lifelong reader, book-lover, and library patron; but prior to my experience with CCL, I had never worked in a library setting, nor did I have any real desire to. My true ambition was—and is—to become an archivist. Seen through an extremely reductionist lens, librarians and archivists differ in that librarians generally work with books and other published media, while archivists generally work with historical original documents and collections. Similarly, librarians generally catalog items and rearrange them so that they may be logically and systematically stored and located, while archivists generally value "original order" and integrity in collections over any cataloging system. This was what I had learned through my first volunteer/internship experience working closely with an historian-cum-archivist at my local historical society for nearly two years. During this same two-year period, I was also fortunate enough to be the recipient of an informal mentoring relationship with Elaine Meyers, head of children and youth services at Phoenix's Burton Barr Central Library. In early fall 2003, these two realms of my experience came together through CCL.

I was about to begin the process of applying to graduate schools. Elaine and I were getting together for one of our regular lunches and gabfests—er, that is, mentoring sessions—when Elaine asked me to describe the work I had been doing at the historical society. I was excitedly describing the steps of "processing" a collection with an intensity that only another archivist could appreciate, when I nearly literally saw a 200-watt halogen bulb go off over Elaine's head. "I think I might have a project for you," she said with the hint of a grin.

To be completely fair, I should point out that while CCL had been one of Elaine's projects for quite a long time, she had only rejoined the Phoenix Public Library's staff relatively recently after working in the private sector for a few years. When I came to it, CCL had survived several changes in leadership, a move to a brand new library building, a lack of funding, and numerous changes in cataloging protocols and technology. Given these circumstances, it is not unfair to say that by fall 2003, CCL presented numerous "opportunities" for an enthusiastic intern. The public and the majority of the library staff were ignorant of CCL's very existence. A handsome group of display cabinets dedicated to CCL in the children's area housed parts of the Center's collection, but were largely ignored by the public. The books and other items belonging to CCL were scattered throughout various public and nonpublic areas of several floors of the new library. Finally, and perhaps most frustratingly, there was no accurate catalog of the items belonging to CCL. What items were entered in the library's online catalog were often extremely difficult to locate physically.

CCL's state was not an unfamiliar one to me. It seems to be my habit to become involved in projects right when they need a large overhaul or re-visioning, so fortunately I had experience in creating order where needed. It was also fortunate that I became involved with CCL just as several other things were happening to improve its fate. For one, Elaine was developing the library's relationship with the faculty and students from South Mountain Community College's storytelling program. With their input, a large collection of folktale and storytelling volumes was officially made part of CCL. This was an exciting and positive move, and added more than a thousand books to the Center.

The other thing that happened was that the entire children's area in the architecturally stunning Burton Barr library was redesigned and physically re-organized. As part of this, CCL's glass-front bookshelves were rearranged from their previous closed circle layout to an open display spanning one whole wall of the children's area. When I arrived, approximately a quarter of the books in CCL were being stored in these cabinets, almost all spine out, as if they were in normal bookshelves, and with no apparent thought having been given to which portion of the collection was stored here rather than in the nonpublic areas. With little over a month to go before the library's annual fund-raiser, "Dinner in the Stacks," sponsored by the Phoenix Public Library's Friends and foundation, Elaine and I decided that my first goal would be to use the shelves to their best advantage by installing a more visually appealing display, reintroducing CCL to the public and our two financial benefactors.

Actually, my first job turned out to be familiarizing myself with the many disparate pieces of CCL and then quickly making major decisions about how they should be organized and presented for the foreseeable future. During this process, I relied on my own experience with organizing small manuscript collections. I also depended on the invaluable advice of the archivist and conservator I had worked with at the historical society, and on Elaine's faith and support. By the night of the fund-raiser, I had moved all of the volumes previously kept in the enclosed bookcases to the nonpublic storage area, cleaned the bookcases, designed a display to introduce CCL to both children and adults, selected books to represent different aspects of the collections in the display, and successfully set up the whole thing.

Soon after this, Elaine and I met with an extremely talented local graphic designer, whom we had chosen to create a CCL brochure. This was my first time working with a graphic designer, and I really enjoyed meeting with her, sharing the descriptive text I had generated, and communicating our goals to her. Most importantly, Elaine and I wanted the brochure to address a wide audience of potential patrons, including researchers, parents, teachers, and potential donors. The process took several months, but the designer used our input and created a brochure that exceeded expectations.

I then began in earnest the hard work of physically organizing CCL. Although similar in principle to organizing a manuscript collection into folders and boxes, organizing three thousand books on shelves and rows was just a bit more physically demanding. The items I had removed from the display shelves had been put into storage as a quick fix; but now I had to reshelve every single book in the collection, and then integrate the newly adopted folktale volumes. The storage area—known as "The Cage" because of the chain-link fence surrounding it—became CCL's official home, and many non-CCL programming items and other miscellany were moved to more appropriate storage areas. A map case, which for some years had been used as a dumping ground for every type of visual display item and poster that didn't belong anywhere else, was appropriated for CCL and moved into The Cage. I went through an enormous weeding process of the map case items, throwing most of them away and tailoring the remaining poster collection to mirror the other collections in CCL. These posters, as well as many works of original art, were then rehoused in the map case. During this period, I often went home very sweaty and covered in dust.

Since finishing that task, I have been engaged in updating the library's online catalog to reflect CCL's holdings. Previously, when patrons looked up an item that happened to be part of CCL, they were likely to see messages such as "CHILDREN'S AREA—ASK LIBRARIAN" and "BY APPOINTMENT ONLY—NO CHECKOUT." Not only were these messages not very inviting, they didn't help the librarian locate the item if someone actually followed the instructions and asked about a book. To correct this problem, several new location and status information codes were created, so theoretically a patron would now be more likely to see "Center for Children's Literature Historical Collection" and "Call Children's Desk." Of course, that meant that someone had to change the codes in the computer system and, since they weren't uniform to begin with, it required a human being to make every change by hand. Therefore, over the past few months, I have been taking every book in the collection to a computer station, where I scan its bar code into the CARL Circ database, updating its call number and location and status information. I also set aside "problem books" for future attention. In doing this, I have found that a staggering number of books in the collection have never been cataloged, are incorrectly cataloged, or are entered by title and author's name only.

Even though the CCL overhaul project is far from complete, I feel a great sense of satisfaction looking back over what I have accomplished there in the last six months. There are two main things that I find very gratifying about archival work. The first is the simple pleasure of taking a jumbled mess and turning it into a usable collection. The other is getting people excited about a collection. Even though CCL isn't technically an archival collection, I am proud that I was able to organize and make it more accessible. I am also proud to report that during my internship I was accepted to several library and information schools, including the School of Information at the University of Michigan in Ann Arbor, where I will begin study in the fall. I also received a sizable scholarship that I attribute to the years of volunteer work that enabled me to present a large portfolio of accomplishments that documented my interest and aptitude for graduate information studies.

As ambitious as Elaine and I were at that first meeting, we knew that I would not want or be able to do everything that was needed, and so we always talked about projects for other students to do in the future. For example, since I have not formally studied cataloging, I will be leaving those duties to a future intern. Also, even though my skills and knowledge of archival principles were very useful while I was organizing CCL, it is a special collection owned and housed in the children's section of a public library and, as such, really needs the attention of library students to make it come to life. This attention is captured in Alicia's story.

ALICIA'S EXPERIENCE

I am a full-time student in the School of Information Resources and Library Science (SIRLS) program at the University of Arizona. I want to pursue a career as a librarian, but when I returned to school to get my master's degree, I was concerned about my lack of library work experience and how that would affect my job prospects after graduation. When I discovered that I could earn six credits toward my library science degree by doing internships, I seized the opportunity. Through SIRLS, I often received notices of internship positions that were open and actively recruiting students. I also had the choice to design my own internships if there was a place I'd like to work and if I was willing to write up the internship plan and requirements.

As a result of my first internship at another local public library, I discovered that I enjoyed working in youth services so much that I decided to become a children's librarian after graduation. Based on this newfound career path, I chose to pursue my second internship with the children's services department at the Phoenix Public Library. I contacted Elaine Meyers, head of children and youth services, who quickly scheduled an interview. When we met and exchanged ideas about our goals for the internship, she shared that one of the main areas of need was CCL. The programming and research projects involved with CCL made the opportunity sound very exciting. I left the interview eager for the internship to begin.

My first day as an intern at the Burton Barr Central Library was also my first lesson in the value of flexibility as a children's librarian. It was the kickoff day for the fall reading club, and several local school groups were at the library for a magic show. Midway into the show, the fire alarm went off and they had to evacuate the entire building. Fortunately, it was a false alarm.

Then, later that day, Elaine asked me to help unpack what she thought was a traveling exhibit of nine pieces of original illustrations to be displayed in the CCL cases in the public area. As we worked through the boxes, we soon discovered that there were actually *seventeen* pieces of framed original art—a stunning collection of collage illustrations from the book *Dear World* by Takayo Noda. I was very pleased to find myself working with these richly colored collages lent by the publisher, Penguin Putnam Books for Young Readers, throughout my internship. My first challenge was finding a place to put the unexpectedly large exhibit on display. Once Elaine and I decided where to put the artwork, it was my job to hang it. With some great advice from the library's exhibits coordinator and assistance from a volunteer, I quickly had the illustrations up and ready for the public.

Soon enough, I began to work on the many projects I had listed in my internship proposal. Most importantly, I was responsible for rewriting the collection development policy for CCL, which hadn't been revisited for over five years and so did not address the many new additions and developments. It was a great opportunity for me to put what I had learned in my collection development course to practical use. It's exciting to think that future interns will be using my rewritten policy to add new items to this already outstanding collection.

I was also responsible for working on a suggested purchase list of original artwork, since a benefactor had recently donated $20,000 for the sole purpose of purchasing original illustrations for CCL. This project turned out to be much more complicated than I had originally anticipated. Initially, I had hoped to see some solid results from my efforts in this area before my internship ended. I soon came to realize, however, that developing this list required a huge amount of research. Fortunately, I was enrolled in an excellent children's literature course while I was working on this project. This allowed me to draw on my newly developing knowledge of children's literature while researching potential illustrators. But identifying the illustrators was only part of the challenge. Not all authors and illustrators have e-mail or publicly available contact information, so getting in touch with them was difficult. My written communication skills have been getting a workout as I write to many well-known individuals in the children's book industry. Despite my efforts, it will probably take several months after my internship ends before all of the responses come in and a formal purchase list can be prepared.

The most exciting part of the internship for me was designing and conducting programming based on material in CCL. I acted as a supervisor for the CCL volunteers, many of whom were retired teachers and artists. Drawing on their wealth of experience and information, the group and I undertook to develop the programming. In the first meeting, we decided to use the *Dear World* exhibit as the inspiration for a series of programs. I continued to supervise the volunteer group as we met periodically throughout my internship to organize and conduct three family literacy events involving collage art creation and poetry reading for students in kindergarten through third grade.

The *Dear World* poetry and art events were a great success. Elaine met with the publisher at a national conference, and suddenly I found myself working on a potential visit by the author, Takayo Noda. I wrote to the publisher explaining exactly what our group had done already, and I helped plan Noda's visit to the library for a day full of events, including an author breakfast for librarians and teachers, a student program for second- and third-graders, and a public sales and signing event. If we hadn't done the programming during my internship, this exciting author visit probably never would have happened.

I gained a great deal of supervisory and project management experience working with the CCL volunteer group, for which I organized and led meetings, followed up on assignments, and served as liaison with Elaine. In turn, I had the benefit of their gift of experience and knowledge in working with children. While developing programming for the art and poetry events, I used and improved my visual presentation skills. I was also responsible for directing the events, which provided my first hands-on experience of working with children in a library setting. Among the things I learned were the value of having a contingency plan for when things go wrong, and that children often exceed your highest expectations.

My internship at Burton Barr gave me the chance to use what I had been learning in my library science classes, while improving vital skills that will aid me in my future library career. I had my first interview for a full-time librarian position before my internship even ended, and I'm sure that listing my internship experiences on my résumé helped me get that interview.

UPCOMING INTERNSHIPS

CCL is an ongoing and developing project full of exciting opportunities for library and information science interns. Although much of the groundwork has been done, the process of organizing CCL is not yet complete. Interns are needed to continue the project of entering basic data into CARL Circ while cataloging the many books that are incorrectly or incompletely cataloged or have never been cataloged before. There is also a need for interns to inventory and more finely organize CCL's many non-book items, such as posters, manuscripts, and artwork. Finally, there is a great opportunity available for an intern to write, design, and potentially set up Web-based information about CCL through the Phoenix Public Library's Internet site.

Even once these discrete projects are completed, there will still be an ongoing need for interns to continue to develop and execute programming by leading a team of volunteers, as Alicia did. There will also be an ongoing need for interns to develop and set up visual displays, as both Alicia and Christie did. Additionally, there will be an ongoing need for collection development through the review of the library's holdings and storage items and recruitment of donations from authors, illustrators, and publishers. Although there are certain goals the library wants to accomplish with CCL, there is also a great deal of flexibility available for interns to focus on areas of the collection that will promote their own career ambitions.

IV

USING INTERNSHIPS AS A RECRUITMENT TOOL

• 17 •

"Recruitment Through Mentoring": Success in Illinois

Miriam Pollack

*W*hat is an internship? According to the University of Colorado, an internship is any "agreed-upon experience in a work setting that is driven by intentional learning goals and accompanied by sustained reflection." Furthermore, an internship, which often corresponds with the intern's course of study, provides a "deliberate learning experience" of mutual benefit to both the student and the host agency (see http://www.colorado.edu/chancellorslrap/lcglossary.html).

Over the years, library educators and librarians have used internships as a means to provide practical experience, leadership and management training, and support and mentoring to underrepresented students. Internships also provide exposure to the demands and challenges of a professional working situation and, thus, offer the opportunity to examine at close range one possible career path. In 1991, the library systems in northern Illinois expanded on the traditional concept of an internship and instituted an innovative model of recruitment for the library profession.

To develop appropriate recruitment models, it is useful to examine why people choose library science as a career. According to a study by Kathleen M. Heim and William E. Moen, called *Occupational Entry: Library and Information Students' Attitudes, Demographics and Aspirations Survey* (American Library Association Office for Library Personnel Resources, 1989), a majority of library school students either have previous library work experience or choose to enter the profession because of contact with librarians. "Recruitment Through Mentoring," a federally funded project coordinated by the North Suburban Library System in Wheeling, Illinois, was developed to address the shortage of librarians statewide in 1991—a phenomenon that continues today in libraries throughout the country. The profession can learn a great deal from the success of this project.

PROJECT BACKGROUND

Although the literature discusses various ages at which to recruit potential librarians—most often stating "the younger the better"—we aimed the "Recruitment Through Mentoring" project at students who were between their junior and senior years of college. In particular, those students, who had a liberal arts background or had not yet settled into a specific career, were prime targets for recruitment. The project provided the opportunity for twenty interns to get a positive, firsthand glimpse of the library profession by working closely with master's-degreed librarians as mentors. We believed that the special attitudes, values, teamwork, and guidance provided by the mentor would encourage the intern to attend library school. We looked for mentors who were enthusiastic about the library/information profession and about their own jobs.

The best way to "sell" librarianship is to show what an interesting and creative job a librarian holds. Therefore, even if the interns chose not to become librarians, we hoped their experience would inspire them to become strong public library supporters or perhaps participate in other ways, such as library trustees or volunteers.

PROJECT BASICS

Our one-year project created a mentor program, pairing potential librarians with practicing library leaders. This provided the contact and experiences that students eventually found so important in their career decision-making. Two previously successful mentor projects were referenced: the Yale University Library program, funded by the Council on Library Resources, and the REFORMA/ UCLA mentor program.

The Yale University internship program, which operated during the summer of 1988, provided undergraduate students with an initial introduction to and exploration of academic librarianship. Each intern worked directly with a technical or subject specialist prominent in the library field in order to promote a mentoring relationship. Interns were assigned special projects, and the mentors acted as advisors. As a result, two of eight interns entered a library science graduate program.

The REFORMA/UCLA mentor program, in place at the University of California, Los Angeles, since 1985, was established to help recruit bilingual-bicultural students into the library profession by matching prospective and current library school students with professional bilingual-bicultural librarians. The primary recruitment pool was made up of Latino/a library personnel, including pages, clerks, and paraprofessionals. The mentor provided a support system for the potential librarian as he or she proceeded through undergraduate and graduate school. At the end of three years, the program had established eighteen formal mentor/intern partnerships.

The "Recruitment Through Mentoring" project combined elements from the Heim and Moen study as well as from the Yale and REFORMA/ UCLA programs. Undergraduates between their junior and senior years were recruited and paired with librarian mentors. These potential new colleagues were provided with the library experience and contact with a librarian that promotes movement into a library science program.

The project's advisory committee, which consisted of eight librarians, reflected a broad range of experience in the profession. All of the members had an interest in the project and some had experience with mentoring and/or recruitment. The committee was used for brainstorming and as a sounding board for ideas as the project progressed. I served as the project director.

RECRUITMENT OF PROJECT PARTICIPANTS

Librarian mentors, who were recruited through a professionally designed flyer distributed to all Illinois library systems, were required to have a master's of library science degree and be currently employed in a public library. We looked for mentors who projected enthusiasm for and dedication to the profession while embodying a broad perspective of librarianship. Toward this end, the application form included questions about their perceptions of the role of a mentor as well as what excited them about their job (see appendix 17A).

Mentors were told that by working closely with an intern they impart a set of attitudes and values, which differentiates mentoring from job training. A mentor, after all, may serve as a teacher, coach, counselor, role model, guide, or advocate.

To recruit students, a flyer was sent to career placement officers of the fifty-eight four-year colleges and universities in Illinois. We also placed ads and press releases in college and local newspapers, which generated many requests for information from both students and parents. Students who met certain criteria were sent application forms (see appendix 17B). The rest were sent general information about the profession or were referred to local library schools.

Student participants were offered eight weeks of full-time work in the summer of 1991. They earned $3,000 while learning about libraries and gaining work experience. We required that the students be seniors in fall 1991 and have a cumulative grade point average equivalent to B (3.0). In addition, they could have no previous library work experience, could not be related to or close friends with a librarian, nor could they have already chosen library and information science as a career.

SELECTING INTERNS

The students who passed the initial screening process were interviewed by telephone and rated on the following factors:

> written communication skills (the application contained an essay);
> letter of recommendation;
> oral communication skills;
> career plans/directions;
> demonstrated interest in the program (simply wanting the money was not enough motivation); and
> what they hoped to gain from the program.

Over eighty students applied. We were impressed and surprised by the number and quality of the applications. The interns brought a wide variety of skills and talents to their libraries. Once selected, the interns and mentors were matched on the basis of interests and geographic locations.

Money was both a positive and negative factor. The salary was commensurate with other professional internship programs and so was, no doubt, a draw for students and their parents. During the interview, we eliminated those applicants who had already chosen another career path.

MENTOR TRAINING

Mentor education began with the application process. Along with a letter describing the project, all applicants were sent an information sheet that described mentoring. In addition, the mentors were invited to a full-day training session to learn about the mentoring process. Led by Maureen Sullivan, a consultant in organizational development, the workshop emphasized how to establish a positive relationship with a protégé, including: mentoring style assessment, understanding the needs of the intern, skills for effective communication, and learning from each other as well as from the project experience (see appendix 17C). Although some of the librarians had prior experience as mentors or protégés, none had participated in such a structured program before.

SUMMER PROJECTS

The model for this project was based on library school internship/work-study programs. The professional nature of the intern's work was emphasized throughout the project. In fact, in their original written applications, the librarians were asked to describe the type of work they envisioned the interns doing. Their answers to this question were important in the mentor selection process.

Mentors were asked to prepare several project ideas to discuss with the intern at their first meeting. Each intern was to have at least one discrete major project that would be completed by the end of the summer. We felt this would help the intern and mentor structure their work days, give them some "time off" from each other, and provide the intern with something to show for the summer's work. We recognized that the interns were developing a résumé/portfolio for future work or graduate school application and felt that they should have a project to talk about. In practice, several of our interns completed more than one major project. Completed projects included:

writing a newspaper column, press releases, and publicity;
assisting with summer reading program activities;
assisting with editing the library's monthly newsletter;
developing library displays;
graphic design;
designing and conducting children's programs;
writing a history in preparation for the library's centennial anniversary;
updating the union list of music periodicals;
indexing the record collection;
ordering records;
verifying book orders;
creating bibliographies;
giving presentations (with the outreach coordinator) at retirement and
    nursing facilities;
weeding the collection;
updating the community organization list;
reorganizing office files;
compiling census data and library statistics;
preparing a subject guide to the periodical collection;
book selection;
leading book discussions;
training junior volunteers; and
reorganizing the paperback collection.

In addition to their projects, interns worked along with their mentors, interfacing with patrons, answering reference questions, attending meetings, etc. Interns were not supposed to just shelve books or do clerical tasks. Because the librarian/intern relationship was the focus of the project, each student worked with only one mentor.

FIELD TRIPS

Thanks to our grant funding, we were able to sponsor field trips to a number of libraries and library organizations during the course of the project. Because the goal was to showcase exciting library innovations of the day, we deliberately decided to visit the *best,* not necessarily the most *typical* libraries. The Schaumburg Township District Library, the North Suburban Library System, and the Follett Library Book Company were all chosen because of their extensive computer facilities. Follett also provided an overview of the book wholesaling business. Visiting the Art Institute of Chicago exposed the students to an interesting special library. The students also got to tour the inside of Chicago Public Library's Harold Washington Library Center while it was still under construction.

EVALUATION

As project director, I visited each library site twice during the summer: once within the first two weeks, and again toward the end of the project. In particular, I checked to see that the mentor/intern match was working and that the student was involved in work beyond clerical tasks. Further evaluation was conducted through written surveys, which were sent to all mentors and interns, and through separate focus groups, which were held at the final celebratory picnic. As is apparent from the survey findings (see appendixes 17D and 17E), the mentoring project was a huge success, with several interns enthusiastically recalling their experiences in the library.

PROJECT FOLLOW-UP

A major element of the evaluation was a two-year longitudinal study to discover if participation in the project had any long-term effects on the interns' career choices. Tracking the interns was done by the North Suburban Library System through follow-up letters. Each mentor was asked to contact his or her intern at least twice during the year following the summer program. Some interns were also invited to visit the library and, in a few cases, worked as part-time employees during school breaks.

The project also paid for the students' membership in ALA, so they received *American Libraries* during the school year. We hoped that this would continue their interest in libraries and also encourage word-of-mouth advertising among their peers. At the end of six months, three interns had decided to go to library school, twelve were attending other graduate programs, and five were undecided. At the end of two years, we determined that five of the twenty students had indeed attended library school. Of these, one student was a person of color. Yet another intern became a member of her public library board of directors.

CONCLUSION

Librarianship is the best-kept secret around. Those who do not know librarians have accepted the stereotype. Those who do know us, however, embrace and support librarianship with enthusiasm. Provide a student with the experience of working in a library, and you have created a librarian, a future library trustee, or a library supporter. During the "Recruitment Through Mentoring" project, we not only raised the awareness of Illinois college and university placement officers but also of the community at large.

As professionals, we must attract and entice bright students into our libraries, mentor them, and demonstrate the best of who we are and what we do—show them the creative, intellectual, and fun aspects of our jobs and personalities. Students between their junior and senior years in college are excellent targets for recruitment. Providing a positive internship experience in a library might just bring them into librarianship.

APPENDIX 17A

Mentor Information Form

Name: _____   Title: _____
Library: _____   Phone: _____

1. What excites you about your job?
2. How do you perceive your role as a mentor for this project?
3. Describe the general nature of the work for the intern. (Consider the work/job as professional. This description will be available and used during both the mentor and intern selection and matching process.)

APPENDIX 17B

Student Application Form

Name:_____

College or University:_____

Current Address (until_____):_____

Permanent Address:_____

Phone:_____

Major:_____ Minor:_____

Current Cumulative Grade Point Average:_____ based on_____

The following areas of librarianship interest me the most:
(You may select more than one.)

____Research and Reference   ____Computer Services
____Adult Services   ____Cataloging/Technical Processing
____Youth Services   ____Administration
____Interlibrary Loan   ____Unsure, need more information
____Willing to be placed as
     openings occur

My faculty letter of recommendation will come from:
Name:_____
Department:_____ Phone:_____

I understand that it is my responsibility to see that the recommendation letter is to be sent by [date].

Only twenty interns will be selected from applications state-wide. Why do you want to be selected for this special internship program?

To the best of my knowledge, all of the information on this application is accurate.

_____   _____
Signature   Date

APPENDIX 17C

How to Be an Effective Mentor: The Mentor's Roles and Responsibilities

The mentor has four key roles:

1. Developer of skills
2. Developer of careers
3. Promoter of professional activities
4. Counselor

To fulfill these roles, the mentor does the following:

1. Determines the particular strengths and weaknesses of the intern or protégé. Reinforces the strengths and offers guidance and coaching to improve upon weaknesses or areas where development is needed.
2. Assesses the potential of the intern or protégé. Does this person have the potential for development and success in this profession?
3. Helps the intern or protégé learn about the important activities, associations, people and events in the profession. Helps the person to develop a network of colleagues who will aid in his or her development.
4. Counsels the intern or protégé whenever necessary. Provides support in difficult times and helps in problem solving. The nature of this help in solving problems is one of exploring options and providing support rather than one of giving advice or solving the problem for him or her.
5. Shares knowledge, expertise, and information.
6. Assists in career and personal development planning.
7. Promotes the protégé or intern to others. Increases his or her visibility.
8. Accepts the protégé or intern for who he or she is. Focuses on helping him or her to develop individual strengths, not on changing the person.

APPENDIX 17D

Intern Evaluation Results

Nineteen of twenty intern evaluation forms were returned. They rated the following items as follows:

Orientation: Above Average, 85%
Mentor/Intern Match: Above Average, 95%

Would you feel comfortable contacting your mentor about career advice?
Yes, 90%
Did the Internship program meet your expectations?
Yes, 90%
Because of this experience are you considering the library profession as a career choice at this time?

Yes, 50%

Maybe, 10%

No, 35%

No response, 5%

What are some of the things you learned about public libraries that you didn't know before?

I didn't know librarians needed master's degrees

I didn't know about the field of library science. I didn't see it before as a career and now I do.

I didn't know how hard librarians work for the public in serving their patrons.

I didn't think of asking a librarian questions. I thought they didn't want to be bothered.

I didn't know the extent of the questions they answered.

Reference is much harder than I thought.

Libraries can be so versatile and librarians can apply all of their knowledge.

Libraries are run like small businesses with promotion and publicity.

Libraries go all out for patrons.

How varied the reference subject questions are—all subjects are included.

I didn't know the amount of work that went into preparing children's programs.

I didn't know how helpful the libraries are—such as dealing with divorced mothers and getting books for their children on the subject.

Libraries serve the whole family and they have a central place in the community.

The extent of community service—not just checking out books.

The library is a vital community service.

What is your perception now after working in a public library for eight weeks?

I took libraries for granted and now am more appreciative of them, they have lots to offer.

The behind the scenes work is incredible; programs, board meetings, reference work, the library system.

The library is never quiet.

Realize what a great resource a library really is and how important it
is to some people.

I had no idea about the controversies, the new ideas, and the politics of
boards and all the new technologies, how "in touch" librarians had
to be with business, social issues, etc.

I would consider library school as a graduate program experience

Describe the internship experience.

Enlightening experience, gained more knowledge and a better appreciation of libraries and what makes them run.

Overwhelming, positive experience.

Unique opportunity to see a public library from the inside out.

This experience intensifies my affection for libraries and has generated
a more enthusiastic advocate of the library as an institution.

Friendliest place I ever worked and enjoyed the hands-on experience.

Although I would not be a librarian, I would support any local library
with taxes.

I never stopped to think before of how important libraries are to everyone.

Caused me to evaluate the important role which a public library plays
in its community.

My mentor and the staff were wonderful.

APPENDIX 17E

Mentor Evaluation Results

- Summary of Comments:
  I thought the experience would be stressful and a drain on my time. I
  was pleasantly surprised because the intern was a bright person who
  needed less training than I thought.

  I was excited and my expectations were more than met.

  It was a very positive program.

  Structured time was spent talking about libraries and the intern had
  good questions about the "big picture" and library philosophy.

  The organization of the program was good. Everything was laid out
  and structured. The notebooks were a big help.

  The quality of the interns was good.

  The interesting thing was the talents they brought with them.

- Suggestions for Change:
  The interns and mentors wanted more: more time, more field trips,
  more information, closer locations for students, more money.

The "Working with Kids @ Your Library" Mentorship Program, County of Los Angeles Public Library

Penny S. Markey

*H*igh turnover among children's librarians is not a new phenomenon for the County of Los Angeles Public Library or any other large library system, for that matter. Since I became coordinator of youth services for the county library in 1980, there has never been a time when our forty-five children's librarian and seven upper-level children's coordinator positions have all been filled at the same time. The children's librarian requires a particular mind-set, special skills, and the ability to be an excellent manager as well as an enthusiastic practitioner. In addition to the natural attrition within a large system, the County of Los Angeles Public Library recognizes the various skills necessary to be successful children's librarians and often promotes them to community manager or other upper-level positions.

In recent years, it has become increasingly difficult to attract and retain children's librarians. There are now more career options for women. As in nursing and teaching—and other traditional "women's" professions—there are fewer applicants for more jobs. Library schools have closed, and those who do receive their master's degrees often seek academic or educational technology positions instead of service in public libraries. The few children's librarians graduating annually have become even more rare.

That this phenomenon is not geographically unique was made clear during discussions with children's services coordinators from other large libraries. The problem of recruiting and retaining children's librarians seems to be endemic nationwide. As a result of those discussions and brainstorming sessions with colleagues—especially Rosanne Cerny of the Queens Borough (New York) Public Library—the idea for the "Working with Kids @ Your Library" program was born.

RECRUITING CHILDREN'S LIBRARIANS

As became clear, it was necessary to recruit not only for our organization but for the profession at large as well. In 2001, the County of Los Angeles Public Library applied for and received a two-year Library Services and Technology Act grant to employ fifteen college students (during each of the two grant years) as summer library workers. It was determined that the students must have completed their sophomore year in college and have a background and/or demonstrated interest in the field of child development, literacy, or education. Our underlying goal was to encourage them to pursue librarianship as a career and introduce them specifically to children's librarianship. This was to be accomplished by pairing the student worker with a "master" children's librarian, thus creating a mentoring situation. The mentor relationship would be combined with hands-on experience and on-the-job training. An additional benefit was to provide the children's librarians with an extra set of hands during the busy summer months.

The project development team consisted of the coordinator of youth services, regional youth services coordinators, and selected mentor librarians. The project team developed a recruitment strategy and campaign to identify and subsequently hire the student workers. The recruitment tasks included identifying and contacting local colleges and universities and creating a job description, recruitment flyers, and job bulletins for posting on physical bulletin boards as well as on the Internet. Tasks included developing interview questions and selection criteria, conducting interviews, and subsequently hiring the staff.

During each spring of the two-year program, the library conducted an extensive recruitment effort among college students by sending packets to thirty-two local colleges and universities. In addition, during the second year, the positions were posted on MonsterTrak.com where the job bulletin was made available to students at more than a hundred colleges in southern California and across the state. (This was the first time that we had ever posted a position using that service.) In the first year, approximately twenty-five students applied to the program. During the second year, however, sixty-three qualified candidates applied and were included on the library's certified student worker employment list. In both years, the students, who were ethnically diverse, indicated an interest in working with children either through their stated career goals or through previous work experience. All applicants were also enrolled in college or university programs. Their ages ranged from approximately nineteen through forty years. Twenty-eight women and two men were eventually selected to participate in the program.

GETTING STARTED

Training for both master librarian mentors and the student workers was an essential element of the program. For the most part, the mentors were the same for both years of the program. The librarians participated in a training session each spring to prepare them for their role as mentors. They were introduced to the concepts of mentoring and participated in exercises to facilitate joint planning and communication. They also worked together to identify tasks for the student workers that would not only enhance the summer program but would provide a positive image of librarianship as a career.

The library deliberately chose to select a separate group of student workers each year to maximize the number of individuals who would participate in the program. In both years, before beginning their assignments, the student workers attended a day-long group orientation and training session designed to introduce them to the public library. During these workshops, they were exposed to the service goals of the library as well as the goals of the "Working with Kids @ Your Library" project itself. In addition, they were given an overview of the library's summer reading program and their expected role in support of that program. The student workers learned the ages and stages of child development and reviewed the books that children of differing ages enjoy. They also participated in program demonstrations, story-craft activities, and readers theater, where performers read aloud from a script. Additionally, they were given the opportunity to talk about their own personal talents and goals as they related to the public library. As a follow-up, they then received extensive on-the-job training. During the course of both years of the program, the summer workers also attended an information session with representatives from the University of California, Los Angeles, and San Jose State University library schools.

WORKING AT THE LIBRARY

Each of the student workers worked approximately thirty-two hours a week for eight to ten weeks during June, July, August, and early September. All but one of the student workers worked for the entire grant period each year. Tasks varied from library to library. Student workers participated in program development and presentation. Some visited schools with their partner librarian and participated in assembly or classroom presentations. Many were involved in decorating their children's rooms. One student worker developed a program participation database. The students were encouraged to utilize their own skills and interests and presented readers theater classes and story-craft programs and did one-on-one read-together programs. Some students managed the library's homework centers and provided year-round or summer-school homework support. The students even participated in system-wide events such as staffing the library information booth at a county-wide family festival.

EVALUATING SUCCESS

Program evaluation was conducted using both quantitative and qualitative methods. Library staff conducted both a pre-test and post-test survey of the student workers (see appendixes 18A and 18B). These surveys indicated the students' familiarity with the public library and interest in librarianship before participating in the program and then again at the end. Focus groups were also conducted with the students and the library mentors. In addition, library staff compared reading program participation data during the year before the program and after. Each year, in late August, the library conducted separate student worker and mentor/librarian follow-up meetings. A facilitator worked with the student group, encouraging them to discuss their impressions of the mentor program, the public library as a possible future profession, and individual experiences with their mentors and the county library's summer program in general.

All of the student workers demonstrated great satisfaction with the program. Moreover, they all expressed delight and surprise over the services the public library offers to children and families. They particularly liked the opportunity to work one-on-one with children and to encourage them to read. An interesting observation was that the library does not publicize itself and its services well enough to the general public. They also expressed a need for the county library to develop a summer reading program with graphics and incentives that appeal more to an older age group (ten- to twelve-year-olds).

The librarian mentors also conveyed their enthusiasm for the program. Although they acknowledged the extra workload that the program entailed, they nonetheless felt that the benefits of having able and eager assistants provided added value to their summer programs and that serving as a mentor was a rewarding experience.

The librarians also found that the student workers, most of whom were in their late teens and early twenties, attracted an older group of summer reading participants. Indeed, many more fifth- and sixth-graders participated than had in previous years. Apparently, the student workers related very effectively with the upper-elementary and middle-school children who looked at them as role models. Also, individual participation in the program was sustained longer through the summer. The librarians felt this was a result of having an extra person who had more time to engage in one-to-one conversations with the children.

How do we measure our success? One of our student workers did matriculate into library school and another one is thinking seriously about it. Although several students still plan to become teachers, all of them acknowledged that, before their experience with us, they had no clue about the resources that are available here for children and families. They also previously had no idea about the excitement and joy the public library could generate about books and reading. Whether the students who participated in the program go on to become librarians or teachers or parents, they will be prepared to introduce the children in their lives to the joy of books and reading through the wonderful community resources of the public library.

EPILOGUE

Next steps. . . . Although the grant ended in fall 2003, the county librarian has indicated a commitment to continuing the program from within our own budget once our funding stabilizes. Staff is looking forward to that time.

APPENDIX 18A

Library Internship Program Pre-test

I have completed _____ units toward my bachelor's degree.
My major is _____.
I have worked in a library (public, school, etc.) before.   Yes   No
I have a public library card.   Yes   No
The last time I visited the public library as a customer was _____.
In the past, I mostly visited the public library to _____.
I participated in my library's summer reading program when I was growing up.
    Yes   No
My favorite children's book is_____.
How would you describe a children's librarian? What is their role; what kinds
    of tasks do they perform?
Have you ever considered librarianship as a career?   Yes   No
Do you think that you would ever consider librarianship as a career?
    Yes   No

What do you hope to gain from your summer student professional worker experience in the County of Los Angeles Public Library?

APPENDIX 18B

Library Internship Program Post-test

My major is _____.
My favorite children's book is _____.
Please rate your experience working at the public library this summer.
    1   2   3   4   5
How do you think that we could improve the program for next year?
How would you rate your mentor?
    1   2   3   4   5
How could your library supervisor be a better mentor to another student if the program is available next year?
In what areas would you have liked to have received more training?
After your experience as working as a summer reading intern, do you think that you would ever consider librarianship as a career?   Yes   No
Why or why not?
Would you recommend this work experience for other college students? Yes   No
On the attached sheet, please give us your e-mail address so that we can be in touch with you during the school year.

· 19 ·

The FILL Project: Using Internships to Recruit at the System Level

Cindy Mediavilla

In early 2001, Los Angeles area libraries were plagued with what one local newspaper called "a vexing shortage of public librarians." Many job openings had gone unfilled for want of qualified candidates and even the world-renowned Los Angeles Public Library was suffering from a 17 percent vacancy rate among entry-level personnel. The reasons cited for the county-wide shortage included "baby-boomer" retirements, an expanded universe of library employment options, and noncompetitive wages.

Not ones to be easily defeated, the directors of the local public library consortium MCLS (Metropolitan Cooperative Library System) decided to take action by voting to allocate $50,000 to develop a way to encourage library school students to pursue a career in public librarianship. The resulting program, called "From Interns to Library Leaders" (FILL), has been highly effective in helping create qualified public librarian candidates.

DEVELOPING THE PROGRAM

Vicki Jenkins, then–director of the Downey City Library and member of MCLS's administrative council, was the first to suggest paying library school students to intern in Los Angeles area public libraries. Her hope, of course, was that the students would become so enamored of public libraries that they would want to work nowhere else after graduation. Her colleagues concurred, and so the consortium applied for and received a federal Library Services and Technology Act (LSTA) grant to launch FILL, a program that places library school interns in MCLS libraries. With my background as both a library educator and a former public librarian, I was asked to write the grant as well as oversee the first two years of the FILL project.

159

The program builds on internship opportunities already made available through the two library schools in southern California: the University of California, Los Angeles (UCLA), Department of Information Studies, and the distance education campus of the San Jose State University (SJSU) School of Library and Information Science. Both library programs offer students the chance to earn course credit while experiencing real-life library work firsthand. But by the late 1990s, student interest in public library internships had fallen off. Public libraries were perceived as being less "cutting-edge" or exciting than, say, art museum or movie studio libraries. Students also complained that public librarians did a poor job of marketing themselves, waiting for potential interns to "just show up" instead of proactively recruiting. In addition, students expressed the need for monetary compensation, an incentive that few public libraries could afford.

With the monies made available through LSTA, MCLS was able to place eighty-two students into a total of eighty-seven paid internships during the first two years of the FILL project. MCLS also paid for interns' memberships into the California Library Association (CLA) and sponsored attendance at workshops and several library-related events, including annual legislative days in Washington, D.C., as well as Sacramento. This combination of incentives has made FILL highly competitive, with students applying to the program a month before each school term begins. Applicants are judged on their writing ability and on their expressed desire to broaden their knowledge of and experience in public library work.

Once selected, FILL candidates are placed in internships where they will be forced to learn new skills—a student with cataloging experience, for instance, might be placed in a reference internship, while someone who has already worked at a central library might be placed in a branch. Intern duties, which vary from site to site, may include everything from assisting with children's story hours to staffing the reference desk to conducting community needs assessments. During the course of the internship, students are treated as colleagues and may even be asked to participate in staff meetings and other professional events. As one FILL alum explained, "I was exposed to many different parts of the library world. . . . I was allowed to attend library board meetings, sit in on job interviews (even asking questions!), set up displays, create tutorials, create bibliographies. In short, I not only was allowed 'to do my own thing' but I was also given the opportunity to see the not-so-glamorous nuts-and-bolts part of how a public library works."

CHANGING ATTITUDES

For many of the interns, FILL provides a positive first experience working in a public library. In fact, all but one student answering a post-FILL survey indicated that they would now consider working in a public library as a result of their internship experience. "I really had no thoughts about working at a public library before the internship, but now I will not rule it out as a possible option," one student related. Another intern, who had worked exclusively in academic settings, confessed that she had no idea what public librarianship could offer before FILL. "I was not aware that my interest in diversity issues could be challenged and fulfilled in this area of library work," she wrote. Even the student who decided to remain in academic libraries said that he would work only in an environment that has "a strong public access policy." This, he explained, "is very important to me and a belief that has only been enhanced by my internship in a public library."

The internships also help students broaden their view of potential jobs. In the first year of the project, a majority of the participants indicated a desire to become either a reference or branch librarian before their internship, with only 31 percent interested in becoming children's librarians. Another 24 percent wanted to work with teens. (See appendix 19A for the survey instrument.) Although the number of students interested in becoming reference and branch librarians remained steady, the group as a whole expressed an overall willingness to work in a greater variety of positions as a result of FILL. As one student enthusiastically related:

> At the beginning of my internship, I wanted to be a reference librarian. Although I have not been exposed to all public library positions, the internship experience made me recognize how much I would enjoy working in a lot of different positions within public librarianship. I'd be willing to try most anything now.

After their internships, 42 percent of the students expressed an interest in becoming children's librarians, while 35 percent said they would consider young adult librarianship. (See appendix 19B for the survey instrument.) Seven students even said that they were now interested in becoming library directors!

The FILL program also helps students refine their career choices, with several interns realizing an interest in only one or two public library positions rather than a whole range of options. In fact, seven students listed positions that they would now not even consider. "I have figured out that I'm not really a branch-type; I really liked being at the central library," one student disclosed. "Also the cataloging/technical services folks were so removed from the public—I wouldn't like that so much."

BENEFITS FOR EVERYONE

Although more dramatic in some cases than in others, the FILL experience usually has a profound impact on the intern's professional outlook. "When I started the UCLA program, I had intended to be an archivist; however, my FILL experience made it immediately clear how much I belonged in a public library," an alum, who is now a children's librarian, explained. "It made me realize that I enjoyed working with children and that children's librarianship was a real possibility for me." FILL also helped shatter the preconceived notions of another student, who spent her internship working in a public library archive. The experience destroyed her "incorrect notion that only an academic library or museum would hold such useful and fascinating historical items." As she later admitted, "It had not registered that public libraries can also be repositories of historical collections and that a local history collection might actually be better 'grown' where the general public can easily make contributions."

The FILL experience has also helped students realize the importance of public libraries in more than just a philosophical sense. One intern noted that, because of FILL, he had gained "a real appreciation for the importance of a public library within the community and the amount of effort involved in providing the varied services the public library offers." He also found it "very instructive to observe how the library fits into and worked with the city hierarchy." A second intern, who had worked extensively in academic libraries, gained a whole new appreciation of librarianship. "In a public library you actually feel like you are answering reference questions that are important to people's lives—as opposed to academic questions for research or student papers," he said. "So you really see and feel what librarianship is about."

The students, of course, are not the only ones who benefit from FILL. Librarians, too, praise the program for expanding their own professional horizons. "Instructing the intern in our work was a review and learning experience for me as well," one library veteran confessed. Many others express joy at being able to "teach someone about something that I know well and love to do myself." For several FILL supervisors, the single most valuable aspect of the program is the opportunity to work with and support a new potential colleague. "Maintaining the connection with students, the next generation of librarians, helps keep those of us in the trenches fresh," a library director said. (See appendix 19C for the survey instrument.)

Indeed, one of the most consistent outcomes of the FILL program is an infusion of enthusiasm and innovation into MCLS libraries. "Students can bring insight and can help keep staff members fresh," one librarian observed. "Our intern challenged my reference staff to think about why we have certain policies which are now being looked at again, and reviewed to determine if they are still necessary or appropriate." Another FILL supervisor credited her intern with rejuvenating staff. "Her enthusiasm was 'catchy' with staff who can sometimes feel jaded or tired with their work," she said. A third librarian noted that "staff find their own outlook and enthusiasm increased by working with someone new in the field." Yet another said that having an intern in the library helped staff "to concentrate on the positives of their work."

FILL site supervisors have come to expect that the interns will be enthusiastic, knowledgeable, helpful, and flexible. When asked if their expectations had been met, all librarians responding to a post-internship survey replied that they had. "It's always a good experience," one veteran site supervisor responded. "As time goes on I realize even more how important it is for the existing staff to interact with these students and be reminded how it was when they were new and excited about working in the library." Another librarian said that the most valuable aspect of the program was that it enlarges staff's sense of belonging to the wider library community. "Because the interns are generally filled with enthusiasm, energy, and a brand-new sense of the principles that guide the profession, we are reminded of why we love what we do and are motivated to do it better."

If the librarians are inspired by their interns, many of the students are equally inspired by their employers. "The most important thing was the active support and participation of the L.A. community libraries and their willingness to teach me as an intern as well as encourage me in my pursuit of a professional career," an intern explained. Other participants told of lasting relationships forged with their FILL site supervisors and how these people have become mentors. Several former interns are still in close contact with their FILL employers and continue to seek professional advice from them. One alum, who now works in an academic library, regularly exchanges e-mail with his former public librarian boss. She was instrumental in encouraging him to apply for a Fulbright fellowship, which he was awarded.

Even interns who decide not to work in public libraries remain impressed by the FILL program. As one alum explained,

> I really loved my FILL experience—everything about it—I loved the work I did, I loved serving the patrons and being able to work both with others and independently. I learned that I can be flexible and that I would love to work in either an academic library or a public library. But what's more important to me is how the community is being served.

Another former intern observed,

> My FILL experience gave me a greater degree of respect and admiration for public libraries and librarians and increased my awareness/understanding of public library issues. Even if necessity dictates that I find employment in a different sector of the library world, I will always fully support the public library mission and contribute when I'm able.

Finally, a surprising number of FILL interns have found unexpected rewards in serving ethnically diverse and/or disadvantaged communities. As one UCLA student stated, "FILL opened my eyes to a different aspect of librarianship, that actually provided me my purpose. If I had not had this opportunity, I may not have ever found my purpose, which is to be active in providing service to underserved people in my community." An SJSU student told how he helped low-income patrons. "Many of the people who use the branch I worked at are poor," he explained. "I was able to put some of them in touch with resources (like the Internet) that they might not have had access to otherwise." A third student, who had previously worked in an affluent area, had an even more profound experience. "I got to observe a totally different community and their library user habits," she said. "It was an eye-opening experience to see how a poorer community uses and appreciates library resources and staff. I was really shocked at the differences. The kids at the FILL site were *so* happy to receive an eraser or pencil, they were reading every day to finish the program and receive all the prizes."

FILL AS A MODEL PROGRAM

Although FILL is little more than a placement service that provides "added value" to both SJSU and UCLA's already existent internship programs, it does manage to distinguish itself in a number of ways. An especially important "bonus" is the monetary compensation that interns receive for working in MCLS member libraries. Although the money is but one of several factors that motivate students to participate, it does go a long way toward legitimizing the project. As one intern reflected, "I think a lot of [master's] students get taken advantage of while completing internships—I am proud of the FILL program for treating its participants fairly." In fact, for some, this compensation is absolutely critical to their participation. "The monetary incentive gave me more latitude with my schedule and increased my interest in a public library practicum," an SJSU student reported. "Without the money, I may have first tried to arrange another academic practicum." A second intern noted that the "monetary compensation makes it possible for students to see the wonder of public librarianship without making a financial sacrifice." As one librarian observed, "Students are always so short of money that offering them a stipend in return for their contributions is such a wonderful incentive for them to get the practical experience they need to make the right decisions about their future."

Offering a salary also adds an air of "professionalism" that the internship experience might otherwise lack. "It adds an element of prestige to the internship that public libraries might not otherwise have," one intern shared, "and helps fight the academic vs. public library snobbery found in some areas of the profession." Others found that the project "helped to raise the profile of the importance of public library service" and enhanced the intern candidate pool. According to one FILL supervisor, the monetary incentive added a particularly tangible value to the entire process. "While we have had marvelous experiences with non-paid interns in the past, the pay aspect can only serve to elevate the quality of the program," she posited. "By making public library internships more attractive, it would seem self-evident that we will attract a higher quality group of interns to this area."

Competing for paid interns and internships often results in a heightened sense of expectation for both the student and the librarian. "It seems that FILL makes the intern and the internship site have higher expectations of each other, which is wonderful for all parties," a former intern, who now works at an MCLS library, said. "It opens doors that might not otherwise be opened." A second alum observed that FILL sites "make themselves attractive to potential interns—I could feel my FILL site wanted and valued me. My non-FILL site was a great internship and I've made great connections there, but it was unorganized. My FILL site had worked with interns before."

Corollary benefits of the program, such as free membership in CLA and being invited to professional events, also adds to the attractiveness of the program. "The great aspect of FILL was the extras—money, attending MCLS luncheons, and Library Legislative Day," one student explained. "FILL is a 'big picture' experience, an introduction to local and statewide library circles." Another FILL alum said she "appreciated the MCLS luncheon and attending the MCLS administrative council meeting—I think those opportunities separate this program from other internships because the interns truly are regarded as future leaders."

FILL TODAY

In August 2003, a longitudinal survey (see appendix 19D) was sent to the first batch of students who had completed their internships in 2001/02. The survey asked them for: (1) their current employment status; (2) the impact the FILL program had on their careers; and (3) their reflective thoughts about the program. Thirty-two surveys were returned.

For the most part, the respondents were extremely generous in their comments, taking much care in describing how important the FILL experience was to their library education and, in some cases, to their future employment. Seventy-two percent of the respondents were happy to report that they were working as professional librarians. Of these, seven were hired by their FILL sites and four work at other MCLS libraries. An additional seven respondents work in non-MCLS public libraries in southern California. Other alums currently work in special and academic libraries—one is the director of a small community college library in Oregon. More than half (58 percent) of the former FILL interns said that the program had influenced their career choices thus far and were appreciative of the skills learned during their internships.

To date, the FILL project has placed 152 library school students in public library internships throughout the Los Angeles area. Although the program is no longer funded through LSTA, libraries continue to participate by contributing a thousand dollars toward the intern's salary. Students, who appreciate the monetary incentive as well as being part of a successful program, still vigorously compete for the privilege of serving a FILL internship.

APPENDIX 19A

Pre-Internship Surveys

Dear FILL intern:

In order to measure the effectiveness of the FILL project, I will be asking you to complete two surveys—one at the beginning of your internship/practicum and one at the end. Please take a few minutes now to complete the following. All responses will be kept confidential.

1. Do you currently work in a library?   __Yes   __No
   If yes, what type?   __Public   __Academic   __Special   __School
2. Have you previously completed one or more internships/practica as part of your library school education?   __Yes   __No
   If yes, in what type of institution(s)?   __Public library
   __Academic library   __Special library   __School library
   __Archive   __Other (please indicate):_____
3. To what extent did the factors below motivate you to apply to the FILL program:
   a. The opportunity to work in a public library for the first time
      __Absolutely   __Somewhat   __Not at all   __Not applicable
   b. The opportunity to broaden current/previous experience working/interning in public libraries
      __Absolutely   __Somewhat   __Not at all   __Not applicable
   c. The opportunity to complete an internship/practicum close to home
      __Absolutely   __Somewhat   __Not at all   __Not applicable
   d. Encouragement by library school staff/faculty
      __Absolutely   __Somewhat   __Not at all   __Not applicable

e. Encouragement by FILL library site(s)
   __Absolutely   __Somewhat   __Not at all   __Not applicable
f. Encouragement by supervisor/library colleagues
   __Absolutely   __Somewhat   __Not at all   __Not applicable
g. FILL information session (either group session or one-on-one with FILL Project Coordinator)
   __Absolutely   __Somewhat   __Not at all   __Not applicable
h. Monetary incentive
   __Absolutely   __Somewhat   __Not at all   __Not applicable
i. Other motivators:_____

4. Would you have been motivated to participate in the FILL program if the monetary incentive were less?
   __Yes, $2000   __Yes, $1500   __Yes, $1000   __No
   Please explain:_____
5. Have you previously considered a career in public librarianship?
   __Yes   __No
   If yes, what type of public librarian position? (check all that apply):

   __Reference librarian   __Cataloger/Technical services
   __Children's librarian   __Automation specialist
   __Young adult librarian   __Branch librarian
   __Audiovisual librarian   __Library director
   __Outreach librarian   __Other:_____

APPENDIX 19B

Post-Internship Surveys: FILL Interns

Dear Student:

Thank you for participating in the FILL program. Please take a few minutes to assess the success or failure of the program by promptly completing the survey below and returning it via e-mail (cmediavi@ucla.edu). All responses will be kept confidential.

1. Did the FILL internship/practicum broaden your professional library experience as promised?   __Yes   __No
   Please explain:
2. If you never worked in a public library and/or never even considered working in a public library, are you now considering a career in public librarianship as a result of your FILL experience?
   __Absolutely   __Somewhat   __Not at all   __Not applicable

If yes, what type of public library position(s) are you considering? (Check all that apply.):

__Reference librarian   __Cataloger/Technical services
__Children's librarian   __Automation specialist
__Young adult librarian   __Branch librarian
__Audiovisual librarian   __Library director
__Outreach librarian   __Other:_____

3. If you already had public library experience, did the FILL internship/practicum reinforce your desire to become a public librarian?
__Absolutely   __Somewhat   __Not at all   __Not applicable
If yes, what type of public library position(s) are you considering? (Check all that apply.):

__Reference librarian   __Cataloger/Technical services
__Children's librarian   __Automation specialist
__Young adult librarian   __Branch librarian
__Audiovisual librarian   __Library director
__Outreach librarian   __Other:_____

4. Has your FILL experience convinced you that you should avoid certain type(s) of public librarianship ?   __Yes   __No
If yes, what type of public library position(s) would you never consider, based on your FILL experience? (Check all that apply.):

__Reference librarian   __Cataloger/Technical services
__Children's librarian   __Automation specialist
__Young adult librarian   __Branch librarian
__Audiovisual librarian   __Library director
__Outreach librarian   __Other:_____

5. Were you able to develop professional mentor relationship(s) with any of the librarians at your FILL site?   __Yes   __No
Please explain:

6. Now that you have completed your internship/practicum, do you feel the monetary compensation was:
__Generous   __Adequate   __Inadequate
Please explain:

7. Would you recommend the FILL program to fellow students?
__Yes   __No
Please explain:

8. Would you recommend the MCLS library where you interned as a good FILL internship/practicum site?   __Yes   __No
Please explain:

9. What was the single most valuable aspect of the FILL experience?

10. How can the FILL experience be improved?

APPENDIX 19C

Post-Internship Surveys: FILL Supervisors

Dear Colleague:

Thank you for participating in the FILL program. Please take a few minutes to assess the success or failure of the program by promptly completing and returning the survey below via email (cmediavi@ucla.edu). All responses will be kept confidential.

1. What motivated your library to participate in the FILL program?
2. Were these expectations met?   __Yes   __No
   Please explain:
3. Were you pleased with your FILL intern?   __Yes   __No
   Please explain:
4. Were you or other staff members able to develop a professional mentor relationship with the FILL intern?   __Yes   __No
   Please explain:
5. Do you feel comfortable recommending that the FILL intern pursue a career in public librarianship?   __Yes   __No
   Please explain:
6. Would you recommend the FILL program to your colleagues?
   __Yes   __No
   Please explain:
7. What was the single most valuable aspect of the FILL experience?
8. How can the FILL experience be improved?
9. Do you have any other comments about the FILL program?

APPENDIX 19D

Longitudinal Survey

Dear FILL alumnus:

We are interested in hearing what impact, if any, your FILL experience has had on your career. Therefore, please complete the brief survey below and return it to me at cmediavi@ucla.edu by August 15, 2003. Your responses will remain confidential.

1. In what type of library are you currently working?
   __Public library (MCLS/   __Special library/corporate
      your FILL site)   __Special library/law

__Public library (MCLS)   __Special library/historical society
__Public library (non–MCLS)   __Not currently working in a
__Academic library   library, but offered a job
__School library   __Not currently working in
__Special library/art research   a library

2. If working in a library, what is your job title?
3. What motivated you to accept your current library job? (Check all that apply.):

__Good location   __Opportunity for advancement
__Good salary   within the organization
__Good work schedule   __Library is fiscally stable
__Job matches career interests   __No other jobs available
__Reputation of the library as   __Other:_____
   a good place to work   __Not currently working in a
                                   library

4. Have you declined any library job offers since completing your FILL internship?   __Yes   __No
   If yes, please explain why:
5. How did FILL prepare you for your current or past job(s)?
6. Has your FILL experience influenced your career choices thus far?
   __Yes   __No
   Please explain:
7. Have any of the relationships you made during your FILL internship proven useful in your career?   __Yes   __No   __Don't know
   Please explain:
8. How did FILL differ from your other internship experience(s) in library school?
9. Other comments?

Recruitment: Miami–Dade Public Library System's Intern/Trainee Program

Elyse Levy Kennedy

> A decade ago, when I drove from library to library making the daily delivery run, I never dreamed I would one day aspire to be boss of one of those libraries.
>
> —Jeffrey Smith, current librarian trainee

*J*effrey Smith began taking classes toward his undergraduate degree after being promoted from delivery driver to library security guard. Now in 2004, he is completing his master's of library science (MLS) degree while working as a librarian trainee, thanks to Miami–Dade Public Library System's intern/trainee recruitment program, which became active in 1998. The opportunity to learn about library service from the inside out was what inspired him to complete his education and pursue public librarianship as a career.

WHO BENEFITS FROM THE PROGRAM?

> After dealing with a divorce and nurturing my young daughter through a serious medical illness for several years, I was finally ready for a career. I had been working as a part-time "page" shelving books for quite a while, and had observed how libraries fit right into my personal belief and value system. The librarians I was working with sort of talked me into it, and I'm glad they did.
>
> —Rebeca Fernandez, former trainee, current librarian I

A community as dynamic and ethnically enriched as Miami–Dade County demands a library system of high caliber. Although Hispanics, African Americans,

171

and white Caucasians comprise the largest segments of the population, there is significant cultural diversity within each of these groups. Of the eighty languages spoken other than English, most frequently heard are Spanish, French Creole, German, Portuguese, Russian, Chinese, Vietnamese, Japanese, Hungarian, and Yiddish. With a service population approaching 2.5 million, the library welcomes over six million visits each year and circulates more than seven million items. A budget in excess of $80 million for 2004/05 supports a main library, thirty-eight branches (and growing), two bookmobiles, and specialized departments such as S.M.A.R.T. (Science, Math, and Reading Tutoring), L.E.A.D. (Literacy for Every Adult in Dade), Jumpstart (story kits for daycare centers), Connections (service for homebound patrons), and Talking Books (service for visually challenged patrons). Eight hundred computers are provided for public use. A staff of over seven hundred includes both full- and part-time employees.

When the Miami-Dade Public Library System began mining its home turf for future professionals, there were two goals in mind. The first was to identify and develop a crop of future leaders. These potential leaders would work side by side with, and learn from, present-day library veterans before those folks clicked the retirement button. The second goal was to create a career path for our paraprofessionals. After all, these were people who already knew and appreciated our richly diverse cultural communities. These two goals dovetailed with the creation of the intern/trainee recruitment program.

In many cases, participants started as volunteers or part-timers. Some were already on track with other plans or obligations; other participants were in a transitional phase of their lives. They already had undergraduate degrees. Coworkers started hounding them, saying "You've got to get your MLS. We need you!" This "push" factor can be very effective. Once they analyzed things, the prospective candidates realized that library work provided a natural bridge that would allow them to utilize skill sets learned in other jobs, such as teaching, management, or customer service. For many, it was a perfect fit.

Other participants spent years on the paraprofessional ladder. They were thoroughly ensconced in day-to-day operational routines. Many had started college but never finished. The intern/trainee program gave them the incentive to pick up those educational threads and keep on weaving them into a career. It gave them a goal to shoot for.

A smaller group of participants joined the program right out of undergraduate school, without any previous experience of working in libraries. These folks have the toughest challenge of all. Not only do they go through a complete acculturation, but they also must saturate themselves with the whys and wherefores of the daily toil. Sometimes the connection between that toil and our lofty altruistic motivation is hard to maintain. This group has the longest growth trajectory.

HOW IS THE PROGRAM STRUCTURED?

> I was working for a record company and had just started taking classes for my MLS when I decided to help a friend in her job hunt. I noticed an ad for trainee, but the completion of eighteen credits was required. I wrote a letter to the personnel director, expressing my interest but explaining that I had just begun earning credits toward the degree. A few months later, to my surprise, I spotted another ad for intern! This time I was eligible, and I went for it. I didn't expect that my efforts to help a friend would result in my own job change.
>
> —Michele Dye, former trainee, current librarian II

The first phase of the program focused on recruiting librarian trainees. Before applying, candidates had to complete eighteen credits (about halfway) toward their master's degree. This was the perfect option for those enrolled in distance learning classes because it gave them a guaranteed job with a salary (slightly less than entry-level librarian) to help defray the cost of their education. The popularity of this program was so overwhelming that it soon became clear that a pre-trainee (intern) level would be beneficial as well.

In order to establish an official new civil service classification, library personnel administrators worked with the county's employee relations department and union representatives to establish job specifications and a written policy. The labor union needed to see evidence of an education process before coming on board. Objections at first included the perception that we were hiring unqualified people at a cheaper rate of pay to save money. We made our case by showing how difficult it was to recruit fully degreed librarians—the vacancy rate spoke for itself. The compromise solution was to hire all acceptable fully degreed applicants before offering positions to students. Another labor union concern was that their membership base would erode. Interns/trainees are not eligible to become union members, and a five-year program completion cap deters them from joining until much later. We presented facts showing that most participants finished the program in well under three years, at which time they became eligible for union membership. In reality, we were giving professional unions a choice between a vacant slot and a potential member. A compromise under current consideration is reducing the program completion cap from five to four years.

In 2000, an internal career path that culminates in librarian status was formalized. Anyone who has been officially accepted as a student into an American Library Association (ALA) accredited master's program qualifies to hold a full-time position as librarian intern. This encourages paraprofessional staffers to continue and complete their undergraduate degrees and provides them with a logical and lucrative follow-up step. As an intern, the employee works alongside fully degreed librarians as they become adept at the duties and responsibilities at the professional level. They are mentored, immersed, and monitored so that meaningful on-the-job experiences are matched with course work. For instance, class assignments in collection development will be paired with a tour and overview of the library system's collection management department, as well as a branch-level orientation to the procedures and decision-making process that are used to select and acquire materials for various age groups and special needs. Management class course work might be paired with shadowing a branch or department manager, along with an exercise in writing a "mock" performance review. Independent study internships are customized to develop skills and knowledge that can be put to immediate use on the job. These have focused on topics ranging from youth programming to virtual reference.

After the intern has earned eighteen credits toward the MLS, a performance review is conducted. If the intern's performance is satisfactory, he or she gets a salary increase and a status change from intern to librarian trainee. At this point, the individual is expected to function with a bit less direct supervision and might even be left in charge of a smaller branch for a brief occasion. Responsibility for part of a materials budget might be assigned, or supervisory duties might be expanded. Finally, when the MLS degree is conferred, a twelve-month probation begins at the librarian I level. Again, a performance review and a salary increase accompany the status change.

These phases—intern, trainee, and probationary librarian I—not only give employees ample time to determine if the profession suits them, but they also give the library ample time to determine whether the employee is capable of functioning in a professional capacity. Students have a maximum of five years to complete the program, allowing them to work full-time while taking courses either online or in a classroom. If they need a break from school for any reason, they can sit out a semester, no questions asked. As noted, the vast majority of students attain the degree in well under three years. Interim performance evaluations document work progress every six months, and grades are monitored to verify that the employee is on track. Permanent civil service status is achieved after the yearlong probationary period ends.

HOW DO WE SUPPORT THE PROGRAM?

The Guilford scholarship and the county's tuition reimbursement program helped me tremendously. Although some of my classes were online, others required traveling to Broward or Palm Beach

County. I was also required to attend two week-long seminars in Tampa. The Guilford award paid for those gas and travel expenses.

—Susan Cesarano, former intern and trainee, current librarian I

Aside from classroom and on-the-job skill building, the students in our intern/trainee program get other support in a variety of ways. The first consideration for most students is financial. Those participating in this program earn salary levels that are higher than those they earned as paraprofessionals. Miami-Dade County employees also are eligible for the county's tuition reimbursement program, where 50 percent of registration fees can be refunded. If a scholarship covers only part of the tuition, Miami-Dade County will reimburse half of the remaining balance. Thus the student can use a variety of sources to cover tuition fees.

In addition, the library sponsors a scholarship, maintained through private and corporate donations that are solicited in memory of Ben Guilford II, our former assistant director. This scholarship provides stipends that can be used for childcare, transportation, the purchase of a home computer, or other non-tuition expenses. In the past five years, there have been nineteen recipients of this award, with each person receiving a minimum of $800 to a maximum of $1,000. Additionally, the library system partners with various agencies to alert students to other financial opportunities. We also encourage and assist them in applying for awards, such as ALA's Spectrum Scholarship, the Institute of Museum and Library Services scholarship sponsored by the Urban Libraries Council, and the ELSUN (Education of Librarians to Serve the Underserved) scholarship sponsored by the University of South Florida.

Workday scheduling requires major commitment and compromise on the part of both the students and their supervisors. While we don't give "time off" for studies, we do facilitate flexed schedules and allow the use of annual leave time. Those who work in a larger branch with seven-day operations and double shifts have more options than those who work in storefronts or smaller branches. But we bend over backwards to juggle our human resources to accommodate people as much as we can for library school. When we have to, we get creative.

Beyond the financial consideration lies the psychological motivation that comes from a library administration that is dedicated to encouraging education of all types. The accomplishment of any educational milestone among staffers is acknowledged and congratulated in "Library Announcements," a weekly online publication. Once each year there is a recognition dinner, sponsored by the Friends of Miami-Dade Public Library System, so families and coworkers can celebrate together the achievement of associate of arts (AA), bachelor's, and graduate degrees. Each person gets a certificate, a round of applause, and a

photo opportunity with the director of libraries. It is one of the most antici-
pated events of the year. In addition, MLS students attend quarterly network
meetings, where they gather at the main library for a breakfast or brown bag
lunch. This is their opportunity to talk to others in pursuit of the same goals.
To further promote communication exchange and bonding, we also invite
their mentors to attend.

Annually, we offer a stipend to attend an ALA or Public Library Association conference. This promotes professional awareness and participation. A very
brief essay and membership in the organization are all that is required to be eligible for consideration. At the conference, a senior staff member is assigned to
oversee the student's experience. A mentorship program, various electronic discussion lists, and a special professional collection of materials are all part of the
smorgasbord of support we provide. An immersion checklist is widely distributed to encourage supervisors, mentors, and colleagues to engage students in activities, such as location rotations, and in discussions about intellectual freedom,
diverse populations, the library's role in the community, and the importance of
business writing, interviewing techniques, and public speaking.

WHAT ROLE DOES THE MENTOR PLAY?

> I try to always model myself after people who do things right. If
> I sense that people on a higher level are open to me, I'll make my-
> self a semi-pest by always asking how they do this or that. I show
> an interest in things and they respond by sharing their expertise
> with me. I've learned a lot that way.
>
> —Ralph Costa, former trainee, current librarian III

There are two levels of mentorship at play: formal and informal. A formal
mentor, usually from another work site, is assigned to each student. Together
they e-mail, phone, or meet as time permits, even though geography may pose
limitations. They also make an effort to work in each other's locations at least
once. The mentor asks about school, projects, and career goals. Using ideas
from the immersion checklist, they may attend a professional meeting together,
work on a joint project, or discuss other library-related matters.

The informal mentor tends to be someone at the work site, often a supervisor, who is involved in the day-to-day activities that may provide a model
for behavior in different situations. The informal mentor may be observed
calming an irate customer or "going the extra mile." Often this is someone
who senses when the student is on overload and says "hang in there" or deals
with a crisis of confidence by saying "go for it."

IS THE PROGRAM SUCCESSFUL?

> My favorite thing is figuring out what the public wants, and laying out an array of services for them to choose from. I thrive on the front line; for me it is the right place to be. I get tremendous satisfaction from exceeding the patron's expectations.
>
> —Katherine Seaver, former intern, current librarian trainee

Utilizing an intern/trainee program as a recruitment tool has been an unqualified success for the Miami-Dade Public Library System. It provides both a path for ambitious paraprofessionals and a haven for converts from other professions. Indeed, one must be quite self-motivated to juggle full-time work along with a graduate school course load and a private life.

The program allows us to target and recruit college graduates, while making us attractive to people considering a career shift from other professions. Although being well-read never hurts, we especially look for individuals who enjoy working with people and who have highly developed social skills. Converts from other careers may also bring political savvy to the job. All of these characteristics no doubt account for the rapid rise of many former students within our professional career ladder. In the past five years, more than fifty staff members have participated in our program. Of those, only seven people did not stay—some moved, one left to attend law school, and two were not successful in their job performance. Seven who went through the program have risen through the ranks to become branch managers. A host of others are upwardly mobile. They are multilingual and multi-cultured. Aside from English, we have added speakers of Spanish, Creole, and Chinese to our workforce. The staffing complement is more ethnically diverse than ever and serves as a proud reflection of the variety of communities within our sprawling county.

Our interns and trainees thrive in the local milieu—they have ties to the community that strengthen their commitment to public service. We are confident that the future of libraries and librarianship will be in good hands and that our intern/trainees will be the leaders of tomorrow.

Index

About the Authors

Bonnie Biggs is professor emerita at the California State University San Marcos and has studied and worked with tribal libraries since 1989. Biggs is former president of the American Indian Library Association and former chair of the American Library Association's Office of Literacy and Outreach Services Subcommittee on Library Services to American Indians.

Keri S. Botello, MLS, is a graduate of the UCLA Graduate School of Library and Information Science. During library school, she completed a yearlong internship in an academic library. She has been the internship program coordinator at the UCLA Department of Information Studies since 1994 and frequently supervises interns in the department's special library.

Denise H. Britigan, MA, is an information services librarian and research associate with the University of Cincinnati Medical Center Library. Formerly, she was reference and education librarian at Hardin Library for the Health Sciences at the University of Iowa in Iowa City.

Christine Dettlaff is director of the learning resources center at Redlands Community College in El Reno, Oklahoma. After earning her master's degree in library and information studies from the University of Oklahoma in 1999, she worked in public libraries for three years as a children's and young adult librarian.

Davi Evans manages the internship program at the Santa Clara (California) County Library and is the children's services manager. She and Nancy Howe are lead trainers for the library's internship program.

Nancy Howe developed the internship program at the Santa Clara (California) County Library and was the program manager when she was the adult services program librarian at the library's administrative offices. She is currently the community librarian at the Morgan Hill Library in Santa Clara.

Elyse Levy Kennedy began her library career as a part-time page, received her MLS in 1979, and is now branch administrator for the Miami-Dade Public Library System. She believes strongly in "distributed learning" and the need to "grow your own" librarians in urban environments. She has written for ALA's e-newsletter *Library Worklife*.

Janet Larson is the former associate director of the Sacramento (California) Public Library. She currently teaches for and oversees the internship program at the Sacramento City College library information technology program.

Lori A. Lindberg, MLIS, CA, is a consulting archivist and full-time lecturer at the San Jose State University School of Library and Information Science, where she is also the faculty supervisor for practicum coursework in archives. She has worked as an archivist/librarian at the Bank of America Corporate Archives and the Oakland Museum of California. Lori is an active member of the Society of American Archivists, in which she serves as chair of the Archival Educators Roundtable.

Penny S. Markey has been coordinator of youth services at the County of Los Angeles Public Library for twenty-five years. She is a lifelong library user. Her favorite aunt was a school librarian, inspiring Penny to volunteer in her junior high school library. Her decision to become a children's librarian came as an epiphany as she sat daydreaming in the Cleveland Public Library when she was an undergraduate at Case Western Reserve University.

Linda Matchette received her MLS from Syracuse University and currently works for the Solana County Library as branch manager of the John F. Kennedy Library, Vallejo, California.

Cindy Mediavilla, Ph.D., MLS, is a library programs consultant for the California State Library and lecturer for the UCLA Department of Information Studies. From 2001 until 2003, she managed From Interns to Library Leaders (FILL) for the Metropolitan Cooperative Library System. Cindy is the author of *Arthurian Fiction: An Annotated Bibliography* (Scarecrow Press, 1999) and *Creating the Full-Service Homework Center in Your Library* (American Library Association, 2001).

Elaine Meyers is currently manager of children's and teen services at the Phoenix Public Library Burton Barr Central Library. Former project director for Public Libraries as Partners in Youth Development, Elaine has worked in public library youth services for the past twenty-five years. She has been active as a leader and program presenter in a variety of state and national organizations and has served as adjunct faculty in the library programs at the University of Arizona and UCLA. She has a master's degree in theater from Catholic University and an MLS from the University of Arizona.

Natalie K. Munn, MA, MLIS, is an information systems specialist and principal at Content Innovations, LLC. She completed her own practicum and then became a full-time employee at the Museum Informatics Project, University of California, Berkeley, where she worked as a programmer/analyst and later had the opportunity to mentor library school practicum students. Natalie is a board member at the Museum of Local History in Fremont, California, and chair of the Alameda County Library's Fremont Library advisory commission.

Jerome L. Myers began his career as a librarian trainee at Brooklyn Public Library in 2001 and graduated with his MLS from Pratt Institute in 2003. While in the trainee program, he facilitated the creation of the PULSE (Public Urban Library Service Education) program to support library school students in becoming the next generation of librarians.

Nancy O'Neill, MA, MLS, has worked at the Santa Monica Public Library since 1976. She is currently principal librarian for reference services. Before going to Santa Monica, Nancy worked in the literature department of the Los Angeles Public Library.

Michelle Ornat received her MSLIS from the University of Illinois, Urbana-Champaign, in 2000 via LEEP, the online program of the Graduate School of Library and Information Science. She is currently a children's and young adult librarian at the Indian River Library, part of the Chesapeake Public Library in Virginia.

Christie Peterson received her BA in anthropology and creative writing from the University of Arizona in 1998. After college, she worked for the federal government for five years while she explored other career options through volunteer work. In fall 2004, she began the MIS program in archives and records management at the University of Michigan. Her goal is to become a professional archivist someplace where she will get to do cool stuff with cool stuff.

Miriam Pollack was assistant director of the North Suburban Library System, 1986–2003. While there she developed and coordinated the "Recruitment through Mentoring" project. She was a visiting instructor at Dominican University Graduate School of Library and Information Science, 2003/04, and currently runs her own consulting company, Miriam Pollack and Associates.

Kathryn Sheppard is a consultant for the South Carolina State Library, where she conducts staff development for public libraries. She previously worked as the development and special events coordinator for the Glendale (California) Public Library.

Isabel Dale Silver, PhD, MLS, is the assistant dean for academic affairs, Graduate School of Library and Information Science, University of Illinois at Urbana-Champaign, where she is responsible for teaching as well as coordination of the practica and internships and other administrative and programming responsibilities. Dale gained fifteen years of library experience, primarily in public library management.

Jill Stockinger, MLS, has been working in libraries since 1984. She was a supervisor of reference and assistant to the director at Port Arthur (Texas) Public Library and is currently the branch manager of the Sacramento Public Library's Carmichael Branch Library. The Carmichael Branch has a wonderful tradition of mentoring interns at all levels of library service, which Jill enthusiastically continues.

Alicia Sugiyama is currently youth services librarian at the North Valley regional branch of the Maricopa County (Arizona) Library District. In her free time she enjoys reading pirate books to her two sons. She completed her MLS at the University of Arizona in May 2004.

Erica Tang is the young adult services librarian at the Santa Monica (California) Public Library. She graduated with her MLIS degree from the UCLA Department of Information Studies in June 2005.

Taylor Willingham is a lecturer for the University of Illinois Graduate School of Library and Information Science and the San Jose State University School of Library and Information Science. She is a founder and director of Texas Forums, an agency that strengthens civil discourse and encourages civic engagement. She remains active in literacy as a board member of the National Coalition for Literacy and as a materials reviewer for the Literacy Program Leadership and Improvement special collection managed by the Center for Literacy Studies.